It Happened at the National

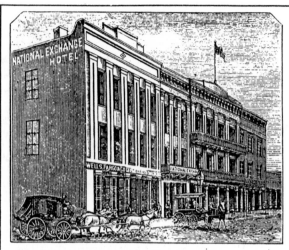

NATIONAL ⚜ EXCHANGE ⚜ HOTEL

AND

STAGE HOUSE.

S. A. EDDY, - - - - PROPRIETOR.

The NATIONAL EXCHANGE HOTEL is the finest structure north of Sacramento—fire-proof, modern in all its appointments, elegantly furnished, and recently renovated throughout. The Table Fare is exceptionally good, and accommodation for families especially provided.

CHARGES TO SUIT THE TIMES. FREE BUSS TO AND FROM THE DEPOT.

Stages leave the House for North San Juan, Camptonville, Forest City, Alleghany, Pike City, Mountain House, Downieville, Lake City, Malakoff, North Bloomfield, Derbec Mine, Moore's Flat, Graniteville, You Bet, Little York and Dutch Flat.

THE NATIONAL BAR & BILLIARD ROOM

Constantly supplied with

—THE VERY BEST WINES AND CIGARS.—

Descriptive.—The NATIONAL EXCHANGE HOTEL is situated on the south side of Broad Street, in the center of the business portion of the city. It is built of brick, fronting on Broad Street eighty feet, and extends back to Spring Street. It has 100 rooms, and is supplied in all parts with gas and water. It is now owned by Col. A. H. Eddy. The National Exchange Hotel Co., a corporation organized Nov. 16, 1863, built it, the main part being completed in the Spring of 1864, and the easterly addition in 1866. The corporation still exists, A. H. Eddy, Edwin Tilley and E. H. Gaylord comprising the Board of Trustees. Mr. Tilley is President of the Board. John I. Caldwell has been Secretary of the Company since March 6th, 1866.

This National Exchange Hotel advertisement appeared throughout the Northern Mine region during Stanley A. Eddy's tenure.[1]

IT HAPPENED AT THE NATIONAL

The Story of the National Exchange Hotel, Nevada City, California; The Center of Town Life for Over 150 Years

Maria E. Brower

Elena J's Publications

GRASS VALLEY, CALIFORNIA

Published by Elena J's Publications
13796 Meadow Drive, Grass Valley, CA 95945
530-272-2119   jim.n6smm@gmail.com

Designed and produced by Dave Comstock

Printed and bound by Thomson-Shore, Inc.

FIRST EDITION

ISBN 978-0-9836867-0-5
Library of Congress Control Number: 2011931152

Cover photo: The California Stage Company moved its office to the newly reopened National Exchange Hotel in 1864, months after suffering major damage in the 1863 Nevada City fire. All of the other stage companies soon followed and moved their offices into the National. This photo was taken sometime after 1897, when the Annex was added on Broad Street, below the hotel. *(Photo courtesy of Wallace R. Hagaman)*

All other illustrations are from the author's collection except the following:
    ix—*Courtesy of Gay Conner.*
    14, 20, 64, 104, 106, 144—*Courtesy of David Allan Comstock.*
    17—Nevada Journal *newspaper.*
    18—*Charles Kuchel & Emil Dresel lithographic firm.*
    33—Nevada Democrat *newspaper.*
    38, 49—*Nevada Daily Transcript newspaper.*
    43, 52, 116—*Searls Historical Library.*
    45—*Courtesy of Max Roberts.*
    55, 69—*Ruth Chesney collection, Searls Historical Library.*
    59—North San Juan Times *newspaper.*
    61, 67, 127, 128—*Doris Foley Library for Historical Research.*
    62, 79—Eleven Generations of the Rector Family in the United States of America *by John Mott Rector.*
    96—*Courtesy of Wallace R. Hagaman.*
    100—The Union *newspaper.*
    115—Nevada City Nugget *newspaper.*
    131—*Courtesy of Julie Bramkamp and Robert Wyckoff.*
    133, 144—The Independent *newspaper.*
    137—*Courtesy of Wayne Teague.*
    141—*Courtesy of Janet Van Dyke.*

This book is dedicated to the most important people in my life:

first Jim, my husband of 43 years;
our three children, Anthony (Tony), Jeffrey (Jeff) and Jennifer;
my daughters-in-law, Patty and Cyndi;
and my four grandchildren,
Andrew, Rachael, Michael and Rebekah,
of whom I am most proud.

If I could give you all one gift, it would be the love of reading—
for enjoyment, for learning and to take you on
adventures around the world and beyond.

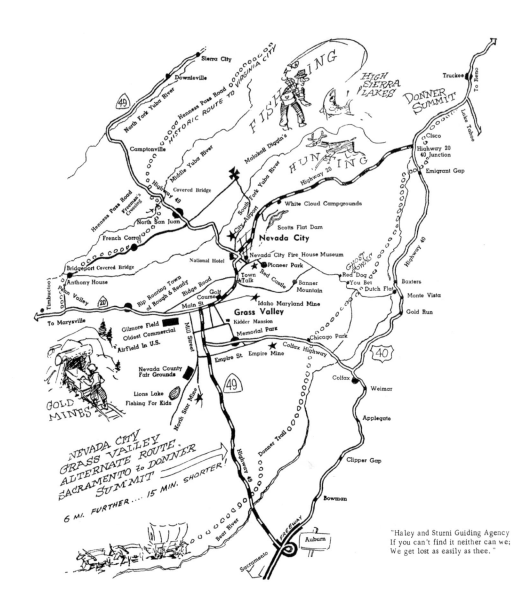

HALEY AND STURNI
Guiding Agency
National Hotel, Nevada City, California
265-4551

Contents

List of Illustrations

Maps

Acknowledgments

I WOULD LIKE TO THANK and acknowledge the following people for their assistance, encouragement and friendship during the years of research and of writing this book, for without it this book may have moldered in the never-ending research stage, (although that is always the most enjoyable phase for me.)

I am grateful to Cathy Wilcox-Barnes, Pat Chesnut, Gay Conner, David Comstock, Steve Cottrell, Marilou West Ficklin, Wally Hagaman, Gage McKinney, Max Roberts, Wayne Teague, the late Ed Tyson, Robert Wyckoff, the staff at Searls Library and Doris Foley Library for Historical Research in Nevada City for photographs and/or research assistance.

A special thank you to Brita Rozynski, for her willing assistance and time over the years, and to long time friends Dorothy Scott and Ken Harris for their expertise and willingness to read a very rough first and second-draft. To my brother Anthoney Woolley for his diligence in supplying his expertise in real estate.

My deepest thanks to my husband Jim for encouraging me when I wanted to pursue other adventures and stories along the way. For attending many "author" workshops and lectures with me at the Tucson Book Festival the past few years.

A very special thank you to Tom Coleman, the present owner of the National Hotel for taking the time out of his busy schedule for questions, interviews and tours of the hotel.

I have learned good editors are worth their weight in gold. My sincere thanks to someone I have admired for more than twenty years, local historian, author and publisher David Allan Comstock, who adjusted his busy schedule to edit this book when he was already knee-deep in other projects. Not only is he a pleasure to work with, but he is probably the most knowledgeable historian today on Nevada County history. When I was writing I sometimes thought, "If only I had a photo of that." Dave often came up with just the right photo to fit in with my text.

Maria E. Brower

Introduction

THE NATIONAL HOTEL IS ONE of the most significant buildings in Nevada City and perhaps the most recognized building in Nevada County.

Closed down by fire once, and surviving several other close calls, it stands today as a landmark which has seen both the glory days of the post-Gold Rush California and the "dull times" that came about periodically, whenever the economy dipped due to falling gold production.

Having been a resident of Nevada County for more than thirty years, I have attended many events at the National Hotel, and since my first visit to Nevada City in 1978 have become familiar with the hotel's important historical significance. The National has always been the center for hospitality and has

The National Hotel as it looks today.

played a conspicuous part in the history of the city where it first opened it doors as a hotel in 1856.

After becoming editor of the Nevada County Historical Society's quarterly *Bulletin* and working at the Doris Foley Library for Historical Research in Nevada City, where I was digging into the old newspapers on a daily basis, I discovered there had never been an article in the society's publication about this historic hotel. My original intent, after researching primary sources, was to publish such a story in the quarterly. I soon found that I had much more richly related historical material than would fill a single issue, or even two or three issues of the Bulletin. My desire to present a historically comprehensive and accurate picture of the National's past has resulted in a writing project which ultimately took on a life of its own.

In researching the many original records of Nevada County—including deeds, assessment records, eye-witness accounts left behind in journals and letters, and editorials and articles written in the many newspapers covering over 150 years of local history—I encountered discrepancies between the information in the original primary records and the oldest newspaper accounts of events compared to the many contemporary stories printed in numerous magazine and newspaper articles in more recent decades.

In 2001 I reprinted the 1856 *Brown & Dallison's Nevada, Grass Valley and Rough and Ready Directory.* This is the first directory ever printed for Nevada County and contained the historical "Sketch of Nevada County" by Aaron A. Sargent, the first history written about Nevada County. This directory is an important resource for anyone doing early Nevada County research. I scanned the original advertising pages for the reprint and also created an index of the names of people and businesses listed in the directory. I was sure that just prior to the 1856 Nevada City fire there was no longer a hotel operating in Nevada City by the name of National. I checked the 1856 newspapers leading up to the fire to be sure.

Finding that almost every article written in the past fifty years, with a few of exceptions, that appeared in contemporary California newspapers and magazines, contained erroneous information about the date the present hotel building was built, the claim of it being "the oldest continuously operated hotel in California" (since 1849, 1851, 1854 or 1856, depending on the article) and the "oldest continuously operating hotel in the West or West of the Rockies, or in the Mother Lode." The last statements have been difficult to prove or disprove when you consider the larger geographic area of the West and West of the Rockies and the Mother Lode. In California alone, many older hotels have changed names over the years, closed and reopened, so that during the time period researched they may not have been in business, or the building had been in use but may have been operated as other businesses other than hotels.

Add that to a contemporary local newspaper article in the 1960s that made the claim the hotel had only been owned by two families since 1880[2] or a local newspaper article that claimed the National has been in operation since 1849. Not only was it not the same National hotel that exists today, the 1849 hotel named the National was a smaller wooden hotel and not located on Broad Street. Erroneous information over the years about the National has been picked up by other newspapers and magazine writers as their only research and make it hard to separate the real facts from incorrect information with those articles now preserved and archived in local history files at the two history libraries and other places. Stories on the National have appeared in *Holiday Magazine, The Oakland Tribune, San Francisco Chronicle, Monterey Peninsula Times-Herald, Los Angeles Times* and other periodicals.

My conclusion is that the National can probably claim to be the oldest continuously operating hotel in California, if not since 1856 (when it first opened as a hotel in the Bicknell Block after the 1856 fire), then at least since 1864 when it reopened months after the 1863 fire closure.

A history of the National Hotel could not be written without including the colorful historical background of Nevada City and stories of the numerous, devastating fires that plagued the town's early years and several near disasters in later years, as well as mentioning some of the key people who witnessed them.

Several knowledgeable historians have written about the tragic and infamous 1856 Nevada City fire, and correctly reported that the Bicknell block of buildings did survive, being one of only six of the twenty-eight brick buildings in the business district to survive the fire,[3] while later writers of local history neglected to investigate the day-by-day first-hand accounts and on-going newspaper coverage of the equally disastrous 1863 fire, with the damage and loss to almost the same footprint (the business district, private homes and all government buildings) that had burned seven years earlier.

The National story has been an ongoing project for me for over eight years, and it has been the most rewarding project on Nevada County history that I have undertaken.

Maria E. Brower   Grass Valley 2011

THE NATIONAL HOTEL

The National Hotel,
In sober, white-frilled gray,
Sedate, respectable and neat,
Lends dignity to all the street
Evokes an earlier, busier day.
Romantic tourists tell
That they can sometimes see
Once famous beauties, frail and proud,
Waving to some long-vanished crowd
From the high, ornate iron balcony.
Or some find in the spell
Of the quiet, shadowy bar,
Shades of the men who struck pay dirt,
Or lost a shirt to a card expert,
And departed promptly, fast and far.
In the graceful dining room,
Where oil lamps cast their shine,
The travelers tell—in a spirit of play—
What they'd do if a ghost should come their way,
And they dreamily sip their sparkling wine.
So their spirits rise and bloom
As they seek their walnut beds;
And if lace curtains stir in the air,
And a boot step falls upon the stair,
And a shadow lurks in the velvet reds.
Will they tremble in the gloom?
Will they cringe and shrink? I think
What some of those tourists would like the most
Is the opportunity to boast
They've spent the night with a gold town ghost!

—B. Tharp

(From the *California Historian*, Vol. 17 No. 4, June 1971.)

Nevada City Ordinance No. 129[4]

Section 62. A first-class hotel is understood to be a hotel entertaining not less than 70 beds. Second-class hotels not less than forty beds. Third-class hotel not less than twenty beds. Fourth-class hotel not less than ten beds.

Section 63. A first-class livery stable is understood to be a stable containing not less than twenty-five horses.

Second-class livery stable not less than ten horses.

Third-class livery stable not less than six horses.

Fourth-class livery stable not less than six horses. [sic]

Passed by the following vote, February 27, 1896. Ayes, Baker, Carr, Hood, Rich. No, Gault.[5]

> D. S. Baker
> President of the Board of City Trustees.

Attest: T. H. Clark, Clerk.

Hotels and Boarding Houses listed in Nevada City and Nevada Township Prior to the 1856 Fire

Names and addresses taken from the 1856 *Brown & Dallison's Nevada, Grass Valley and Rough and Ready Directory.*

American Hotel (probably on African Hill)

American Market & Hotel, Main St.

Arcade House, 6 Commercial St.

Broad St. Hotel, 101 Broad St.

Frisbie's Restaurant & Boarding House, 4 Coyote St.

German Hotel, 12 Main St

Half-Mile House, Shingle Hill

Hotel de Paris, 73 Broad St.

Metropolis Hotel, 35 Main St.

New York Hotel, 92 Broad St.

Oriental Hotel, 16 Main St.,

Pacific Restaurant & Boarding House, 2 Main St.

Ray & Carroll Boarding House, Washington St.

Ross' Restaurant & Boarding House 37 Commercial St.

Selby Flat Hotel, Selby Flat

Union Hotel, 25 Broad St,

United States Hotel, 92 Broad St.

Virginia House, Corner of Broad & Bridge Sts.

Yankee Blade Hotel, 42 Commercial St.

Nomination for Registration of the National Hotel with the National Register of Historic Places

(This information has been extracted from the official Inventory–Nomination form prepared in September 1970 by Mrs. Leland S. Lewis, chairman of the Nevada County Historical Landmarks Commission)

Description

This is the most imposing building in the business district of Nevada City. Three stories tall, extending about 100 feet along the main street, it possesses dignity, charm and an elegance which must have satisfied yearning for "civilization" in the old days. The brick walls are painted dark green which contrasts strongly with the white painted window frames and the many elaborate ornamental features. A handsome wood portico extends along the street front, supported by bellied wood columns at the curb and cast iron engaged columns of the building. About this portico heavy brick pilasters run through the second and third stories, dividing the tiers of windows in a design nostalgically classic. The pilaster capitals are formed with brick dentils, the brick cornice is playfully modeled with metopes; all features being brought out with the white paint. The length of the front is curiously divided into four sections, alternately wide and narrow; the wide ones emphasized by ornamental cast iron railings at the third floor level. Office and shops occupy the entire street floor level, except for entrances to the hotel dining room the bar and to a stairway leading to the hotel proper and the second and third floors. The hotel lobby is a second floor level. At the rear of the building, the ground is at the second floor level and from the side, the hotel is entered through a charming garden. The rooms, shops and all interiors are high ceilinged, well proportioned and fitted with good doors, windows and wood work of the period.

—Francis Lloyd, A.I.A. P.O. Box 177, Cedar Ridge, CA 95924

History

This complex was built for Dr. Bicknell, a dentist, by a Mr. Todd who planned it and supervised the Construction. According to an announcement in the *Nevada Journal*, April 25, 1856, Bicknell's Brick building on Broad Street was completed." In both design and perfection of work it is the finest brick structure in the mountains and reflects great credit upon Mr. Todd who planned and finished it. "Bounded on either side by other buildings (Z. P. Davis's shooting gallery and Thomas/Young grocery) the Bicknell buildings came through the July

19, 1856, fire practically unscathed. Less fortunate was the U.S. Hotel – located on the corner of Pine and Broad – which burned to the ground. The owners of that hotel promptly leased the "Bricknell Block" and on August 20, 1856, opened for business as the National Exchange Hotel.

Historical Significance

It is one of the seven oldest structures extant in the city's business district. It is the only building, in this early group that has been used for the same purpose which continues today. The National Exchange Hotel in operation since August 20, 1856, is one of the longest continuing hotels in the state.

Community Significance

The hotel offered much impact to the business community and local economy in its telegraph service and its freight and passenger services. Its hotel facilities benefited all travelers both commercial and pleasure. It has been the hub of Nevada City's commercial and social life for more than a century.

Architectural Significance

In its exterior the building offers an example of an original building designed in 1856. The interior, though essentially original as to the structural walls has undergone certain rearrangement. The present dining room and bar occupy space once used by the telegraph office, the passenger and freight service and the original dining room. The hotel lobby was relocated on the second floor and the original ground floor lobby converted to offices. The hotel annex built in the 1890 period connected to the hotel at second story level by a glass encased passage way. The annex and hotel proper separated by a narrow bricked driveway known as "hotel alley." The annex was torn down in 1968 and though less than historical its demolition has rendered great loss to the visual effect of the hotel and its adjoining property.

1. Early History of Hotels, Inns and Roadhouses in the West

FROM THE ORIGINAL EXPLORERS to the settlements established in America by white non-Native people in the 1600s, early settlements were made a short distance from either the Atlantic or the Pacific Oceans. For the first two-hundred years the land occupied by settlements was within one-hundred miles of the Eastern coastline. Following those two centuries, the population slowly expanded westward into the wilderness. Therefore, there was a continuous new frontier that was, in the beginning, sparsely populated and isolated from the nearest towns or settlements. As these pioneers and immigrants ventured west to claim land that was often purchased "dirt cheap" (and in some instances free) in exchange for settlement and/or making annual improvements to the land, the early settlers living on the far edge of society often found themselves hosts and innkeepers to travelers passing through seeking food and shelter for the night. For the most part hospitality was given, and most often offered readily, without thought of charging a stranger for lodging, food, water and even provisions for the traveler's animals.

An early Texas pioneer recounts that no one ever considered

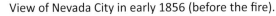
View of Nevada City in early 1856 (before the fire).

charging a stranger for lodging; in fact, it was deemed an insult to offer to pay for bed and board.[1]

The hospitality given to strangers often benefited the hosts as well as the travelers. Living far from towns and busy with daily work on a farm or ranch, little time was left for visiting neighbors, or time allowed for frequent absences away from the homestead. Most hosts were happy for the company and news from nearby towns or news from far away, the East, North and South.

Likewise, in pre-Gold Rush California, the vast area that was colonized by Spain before Mexico won its independence in 1821, Western hospitality by the distantly-scattered California *rancheros* was offered willingly and graciously. Travelers were offered hospitality by people who had been brought up in the Spanish-Mexican tradition of *hospitalidad*, and strangers and friends alike were offered whatever was available, be it an unpretentious adobe *casa* or a large sprawling *rancho* that comprised thousands of acres of rich land. This often included the loan or gift of horses to ride, while the visitors enjoyed the spacious accommodations of the larger landowners. Most often the visitors were welcome, and the stays could turn into lengthy ones, as travel was tedious.

The California Gold Rush changed the slow progress of expansion across the country and the typical gradual settlement and immigration of the West. Prior to 1849 there were "less than a score of so-called 'hotels' scattered among the principal communities of the state, and at the time there was no reason to suppose that their number would be increased. . . . However, when in February of that year the steamer *California* dropped her anchor in the bay of San Francisco and landed the first contingent of Forty-niners, the great Gold Rush was off to a flying start."[2]

Soon thousands followed, rushing to California via the quickest method they could afford; by ship, wagon, horse and oxen. Some even walked across the country to get to California. Just as quickly, saloons, inns and hotels for profit sprang up to accommodate the customer willing to pay usually outrageous prices for a bed (often just a canvas hammock or mattresses on shelf-like perch, stacked two and three in high) and a meal that was usually unappealing—and sometimes barely palatable.

2

Nevada County

When California was admitted as a state on September 9, 1850, the area that would become Nevada County was part of the then very large county of Yuba, one of the seventeen original counties. In 1851 John Anderson and John Wadsworth went to San Jose, the state capitol at the time, as a special delegation representing the citizens of Nevada City, Grass Valley, Rough and Ready and other nearby settlements that had grown from gold camps to "urge the Legislature the importance of immediate action with reference to the proposed division of this county."[3]

It was stated that within the boundaries of the proposed county of Nevada the population was larger than any in the state, and the citizens wasted time in useless and expensive trips to the county seat at Marysville to conduct business. Apparently, a major complaint about "trying to obtain justice in courts so far from home" needed to be rectified. It was also stressed that the taxes paid by the local citizens did not benefit them, but instead helped only those living in Marysville, the county seat of Yuba County.

A Town is Born and with it a Hotel

After James Marshall's discovery of gold on January 24, 1848, at Sutter's Mill, located on the banks of the American River at Coloma in El Dorado County, the subsequent Gold Rush of 1849 soon brought thousands of men, and a small number of women, to California and to the foothills of the Sierra Nevada range. Men flocked to the waterways, probing every river, creek, stream and lake bed in search of gold in what would become known in the northern part of California as the Northern Mines.

There were white settlements in the area that would become Nevada County as early as summer of 1848 at the southwestern end of the county, and in the early spring of 1849 a party of mountaineers from Oregon led by Caleb Greenwood followed the waters of the South Yuba up into the higher country. They searched for gold as far upstream as what soon became the towns of Washington and Jefferson. Today only the former has survived, seventeen miles above Nevada City, while the later town has disappeared. In the fall of that year other emigrants began arriving, swelling the population to thousands.

In October of the same year Dr. A. B. Caldwell built a log store on Nevada Street back of Main Street ravine. From this structure the place was first known, till long after as "Caldwell's Upper Store"[3] and/or Deer Creek Dry Diggins, but eventually the miners decided that the booming settlement and gold camp deserved a better name, and the name chosen was Nevada. That winter was very severe and the heavy snowfall prevented mining activities until the next spring. Other traders and settlers came during that time, and small settlements began to crop up throughout the county, the three largest being Nevada, Grass Valley and Rough and Ready.

Pioneer Roadhouses in Nevada County

Apart from the settlements that would become towns, the first places that offered lodging and food to strangers were the early pioneer roadhouses spread across the county, some in isolated spots. Many were built at a turnpike or toll bridge road and took on the name of the proprietor, or were named for a physical characteristic or local designation. The old Zinc House (destroyed by fire in 1878), Seven-mile House, Half-mile House, Half Way House, 18 Mile House, Six Mile House, Central House, Junction House, Mountain House, and Five Mile House are just a few of the names that are familiar by reading the early newspapers of Nevada City and Grass Valley.

The once well-known Central House (not to be confused with the Central Hotel) was located about half-way between Nevada City and the town of Washington, and was an early stopping-place for teamsters in the old days. The Hunerfauth family, early German pioneers who settled in Nevada City in 1852, moved to the town of Washington and went into the hotel business there, building the original (oldest) Central House between the two towns. That building, which burned down in May of 1873, had recently been managed by John Robinson. In 1885 Andrew Husom, a sawyer previously from Norway, then living in Grass Valley, purchased it and leased it back to Mrs. Anna Robinson, wife of John Robinson. In 1890 Chris Galbraith purchased it and that building burned down about 1901, but Galbraith rebuilt it and that house too was destroyed by a fire in 1908. Galbraith could not call for help because the telephone office was located in the Central House. It is believed that he may have rebuilt the place. The coming of auto trucks "spelled its end." In 1930, when the property was purchased by the Nevada City Ski Club and the old barn was refurbished, it was successfully used for a time as a clubhouse and for winter sports. After a time of inactivity fire visited the building again, and on February 22, 1934, it was destroyed. The ski club did not have the heart or the money to rebuild it. Later the property was sold to Max Lantz, and he erected a new 30' x 24' building constructed of "Cheplin Log siding" that resembled peeled logs in the style of old log cabin construction. The main room had a dance floor and bar on one end and living quarters on the other, with the interior walls and ceiling finished in knotty pine. Lantz' plans were to again make it a winter resort and to have dancing on Saturday nights.

Anyone who has lived in the area for any length of time is familiar with the updated building known as the Five Mile House, currently a restaurant, located five miles beyond Nevada City on Highway 20 before the Washington turn-off. The Half Mile House was located between Nevada City and Grass Valley and built by a pioneer family named Sweney or Sweeney from New Jersey.

There are a number of other road names in Nevada County from the early days, when there were roadhouses and watering stations there to serve travelers.

By 1850 there were 1,000 men mining on part of the South Yuba River not far from Nevada (City). It was during 1850 that two different companies of men formed water and ditch companies to take water from both Rock and Deer Creeks to the gold camps below (Nevada and Rough & Ready) and to Coyote hill, where men were mining at the newly discovered "Coyote lead," but had to haul the dirt and rocks great distances in buckets or wheeled wagons to be washed in the nearest water source at Deer Creek.

1850 was a year of tremendous growth, with the U.S. Federal Population Census for the town of Nevada showing 1,067. By fall and winter the estimated population of the town and outlying area was estimated to be 10,000 to 12,000.[5] In December a United States post office was established under the name of "Nevada City."

By this time Nevada had several hundred stores, houses, saloons and hotels. A large number of cabins were also erected, and those not financially able to put up a cabin or a wooden and canvas structure made do with pine boughs and branches that made a crude shelter.[6] Men were not going to waste time building something more substantial than necessary if they were going to soon move on, or waste valuable time constructing more substantial living quarters when they might miss out on a rich strike. It was a time when the majority of the miners were on the move, and from one day to the next were apt to seek a better location or move to another county if there was a rumor of a "rich strike" over the hill, down a road or up a creek or river.

The Sweetland store and hotel as it appeared in 1939. The town of Sweetland (named for the three Sweetland brothers) in Nevada County was settled by 1850 and in 1860 boasted a store, saloon, saw mill and Brown's Hotel.

2. Nevada City Fires and Town Growth

MOST EARLY GOLD RUSH TOWNS were susceptible to the same fate, disaster by fire. The early settlers and miners quickly built wooden buildings that often shared common walls or were built very close together. Large masses of people living in a small area in an era when wood stoves, and oil lamps, candles were in use and black smith shops were located in the main part of town, and fire suppression and equipment for fighting fires almost non-existent, offered all the ingredients for disaster.

Nevada City was not exempt, but probably not any more unlucky than other early California mining towns. Prior to 1863, Nevada City had suffered major damage from fires in the years 1851, 1852, 1854, 1855, 1856, 1858, and two fires in 1862. In looking at each instance of fire, the values of the property loss reported after the fires (not to mention the loss of ten lives in the 1856 fire, possibly more), the contemporary reader has to have an understanding of the economy that was unique to California as a result of the Gold Rush, beginning in 1849, and later the impact of placer and quartz mining in the Northern Mines. In the early 1850s, although structures were not substantial the abundance of stock-on-hand was.

Fortunes were lost in a matter of minutes by flames that would be out of control as soon as they licked the tinder-dry wood and lumber and could consume an entire town in under an hour if there was a wind to spread the burning embers, to the next building, across the street and up and down each block.

In California during the early Gold Rush years, the cost of goods, services and real estate was determined by how much the market could bear—the scarcity of the goods, the amount of gold being taken out of local lakes, rivers, streams and creeks, and the cost of getting it up into the foothill towns. The prosperity, and lack of it (termed "dull times" by the locals) and the affect it had on the economic conditions of the towns and camps varied,

7

and prices rose and fell accordingly. Unlike any place else in the U.S.—it could be month-to-month, week-to-week, and in some instances on a daily basis due to the great quantities of gold panned and mined in one camp, town or waterway. These micro-economies affected what you paid that day, regardless of what merchants paid for the goods. If men couldn't get rich by mining, they could get rich by mining the miners. Many men (and a few women) found that they could make their fortunes much easier and faster than panning for gold supplying the miners with all necessities and luxuries you wouldn't expect to be available in the isolated mining towns and camps of California.

A Gold Camp, a Village, a Town and a City

1851 was in a period of "flush times" for Nevada City. Money was made fast—as the gold seemed to flow like the creeks and poured in from in from every hole, crevice and stream. Prices were exorbitant then, as in every gold camp, but the miners paid, since their existence depended upon having both provisions and tools with which to work, With more than 10,000 men in and around the town of Nevada, and with most transactions conducted in bags or pinches of "dust," and no one doing any accounting, there was no way to determine the actual amount of gold that was found. The first year it was almost impossible for any man who tried his hand at mining not to find the rich nuggets or dust that had been lying submerged or buried, waiting to be found. The first part of the year there were no banks, and most people had no locks on the doors, or doors on their tents, and no need to do so. The town was almost crimeless, but that would not last much longer. As the next wave of would-be-miners arrived in California they included ruffians, criminals, gamblers and other undesirables for whom many former places of residence had happily paid the outbound passage on a ship bound for California— via a one-way ticket.

The history of the National Hotel parallels the history of the gold camp that grew into the town named 'Nevada' and finally became the small city. To call it a city in those early days was a *bit* pretentious, but for the time and place when nearby towns and gold camps were christened with names such as Little York,

8

Rough and Ready, Hangtown, Red Dog, God's Country, Gouge Eye, Blue Tent, Washington, Jefferson, Alpha and Omega, adding "city" to the early town of Nevada was plausible. With structures constructed from tree limbs, brush, canvas, tents, log huts and shingle shanties scattered everywhere, radiating out from the center of town, it did not resemble a city in the truest sense.

The first hotel was set up under a canvas roof with a sign made from lamp-black on a piece of cloth. The second hotel was created from the seat of a buckboard set upon two tree stumps and the family wood stove moved out of their wagon and set under the canopy of a large pine tree. After all, at the onset of the Gold Rush the land was a wilderness belonging to a foreign country, and most men never intended to settle in the place called California. Maybe one out of several hundred ended up being a permanent resident of the town. Most of those who came to the gold fields had never heard the name of California before the loud cry of gold was heard echoing around the world.

As the population of the place increased, word spread quickly up and down the gold camps of the richness of the area, and men descended upon "Caldwell's Upper Store" or "Deer Creek Dry Diggings" (early names by which it was known) by the hundreds and thousands. In March of 1850 an election of an *alcalde* was held to have someone with the authority to punish crime. It was after this election that a group of men adjourned to dinner at the cloth hotel of Womack and Kenzie located at the corner of Commercial and Main streets. It was said that champagne circulated freely and those assembled agreed that the town deserved a better, more substantial name. Aaron A. Sargent, in his "A Sketch of Nevada County," wrote that each person there submitted names on slips of paper and they were collected and referred to a committee of the whole for selection of the best names. The name of Nevada, suggested by O. P. Blackman, (an early-day merchant), on being read, was immediately adopted by the meeting members.

Contemporary local historian and writer David Comstock annotated a reprint of Sargent's historical account, *1848–1851: 150 Years Ago,* for California's Sesquicentennial in 1998, giving the following information:

Sargent did not come here until September 1850 and therefore had to rely on other accounts [of the early history]. On April 18, 1869, the *Nevada Transcript* said Charles Marsh was "the only person now a resident of this city who was present at the meeting" that named the city, which Marsh said had occurred on April 17, 1850 (not March, as Sargent had reported). Marsh said O. P. Blackman (who had left Nevada County in 1855, and resided in Vermont in 1869) had proposed the name. But in 1878, two years after Marsh died, Blackman's former partner, Edward H. Truex (who had left California in 1851), wrote the *Transcript*: "I have the honor of saying that I founded Nevada City. In 1850, I pitched a tent on Deer Creek Dry Diggings. There sold the first pound of goods. Afterwards built the first house and named Nevada City when I opened the first store, a log house." Survivors have the last word!" [1]

Blackman and Truex were partners in a dry goods and clothing store until 1853. [2]

On November 18, 1850, a petition signed by 219 residents to incorporate the "City of Nevada" was filed with the Yuba County clerk. On December 12 the local post office was officially named "Nevada City" by the federal government. The legislature incorporated the "City of Nevada" on March 13, 1851, two days after Nevada burned to the ground. The citizens petitioned the legislature for a repeal of charter and on February 14, 1852, Governor John Bigler signed the repeal bill. On January 5, 1854, Nevada was incorporated by the Nevada County Court as a "town" under the name of "Nevada City." This incorporation was later deemed invalid and was repealed. On April 19, 1856, it was again incorporated as the "City of Nevada" by the state legislature. Incorporation was made again in 1878.

Tallman Rolfe, editor of the *Nevada Democrat* newspaper, expressed the feelings of his community when he wrote on October 26, 1859:

It is earnestly to be hoped that the people of the western part of Utah will adopt some other name than "Nevada" for their proposed new Territory. Let them adopt the name of some Digger Indian, or any name rather than that of a populous county, immediately adjoining their borders.

If the residents themselves will not agree to change the name, then the citizens of Nevada county should petition Congress to adopt some other name for the new Territory whenever a Territorial government is established.

On November 23, 1859, the *Democrat* editor protested again: "If the people of Western Utah would adopt an appropriate name for their proposed Territory, it would be adopted by the California papers; but papers will not use the name 'Nevada,' for the reason that it is liable to be confounded with the county and town of that name in California." Unfortunately, his plea went unheeded.

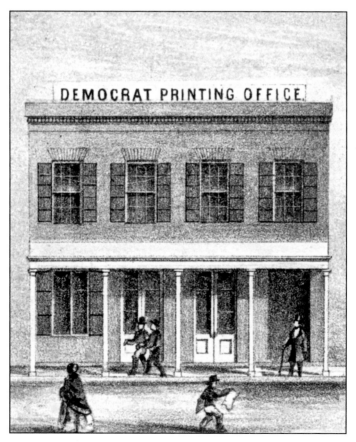

The Broad Street office of the *Nevada Democrat* newspaper as it appeared before the 1856 fire.

3. The First Hotel Named the National—and the Phelps' Hotel

THE PRESENT LARGE BRICK BUILDING named the National Hotel in Nevada City should not be confused with an earlier and smaller wood-frame structure that became a hotel named the National and operated for a short time in Nevada's early history. There were three other "National" hotels not too distant from Nevada City: at Grass Valley and North San Juan[1] in Nevada County, and at Auburn[2] in Placer County. The name has been a popular one for hotels, not only in the U.S. but world-wide, for the last three centuries.

David Phelps and his wife arrived at Nevada after crossing the plains, and Mrs. Phelps is mentioned in several reminiscences by writers who were there at the time and they speak well of her. In the early days she opened a business and was thereafter busy from the very first hour of opening her door. She'd brought a cooking stove with her, so shortly after arriving she opened a pie house and she sold pies made from dried apples for one dollar each, along with coffee at ten cents a cup. She soon purchased two cows and sold milk for a dollar a pint, adding half water.[3] She was constantly busy, and on Sundays when the miners came to town she often found it impossible to supply the great demand no matter how many pies she baked. As soon as her pies came out of the oven they were eaten. Several writers have claimed that she was the first woman in Nevada City.

By September 1851 Phelps owned a dairy, and operated the Phelps' Hotel on lower Main Street on the south side of Deer Creek. His Milk Depot was at the Main Street bridge; and the combination was also known as the Express Hotel & Milk Depot. In February of 1852 Phelps had enlarged his dining room and made other improvements to his building and expanded his business to take on boarders and travelers offering them room, board and milk by the glass (12 cents) or by the quart (50 cents). In July he changed the name of his place to the National Hotel and the editor of the *Nevada Journal* ran a small article on the name change and remodel of the former Express Hotel.

> NATIONAL HOTEL.—The old house known as the Express Hotel by Mr. Phelps has been re-fitted or rebuilt, we should say, and opened under the name of the National Hotel. This house is now perhaps the neatest of the kind in Nevada, and in fact has but few superiors, if any, in the mountains of California. The furnishing is neat and tasty and everything made comfortable.[4]

On September 7, 1852, a fire broke out in the kitchen of Phelps' National Hotel.[5] The flames quickly spread to both sides of Deer Creek, destroying Adams & Co. Express, the Deer Creek Hotel, National Stables and several other buildings. The 1880 *History of Nevada County* gives the number of buildings destroyed by that fire as twelve, but newspaper articles of the time estimated the loss of buildings to be twenty-four. Many of the occupants of Phelps' hotel escaped from upper windows. Although the hotel was constructed of wood and highly combustible, the location of the fire and unusual circumstances prior to the fire may have saved most of the town from burning.

The damage would have been much worse except for fate and the heavy late-winter/early-spring flood of March 3, 1852. As the rains continued over a period of days, Deer Creek became swollen from the streams flowing down from the mountains. The first sign of trouble came when water rose up over the bank and completely surrounded a house. On March 6 the Broad Street bridge was carried away by the fast moving, swirling waters, carrying with it heavy logs and timber that had been swept in the torrent. It soon took out several buildings, including the remaining pillars of the year-old Jenny Lind Theatre and the Illinois boarding house adjoining the theatre. As a result of this flooding a gap was left where the buildings had been swept away, which fortunately stopped the fire from spreading across the creek and prevented the whole town from being destroyed.[6]

Phelps told the newspapers he intended to rebuild on the same site, but by October 9, 1852, he had taken possession of the former Gregory House, where the quartz miners of the Nevada district met at what he again called the Phelps' Hotel on the town side of Deer Creek. Thus the first National hotel made its exit from Nevada City.

In April 1853 Phelps sold his hotel to William C. Asher, one of the earliest citizens of the town. Asher had kept the name of Phelps' Hotel after he purchased it. Asher also owned a ranch, built the new Phoenix Saloon on the other side of the creek, and was part owner of Asher and Fisher's ice cream saloon. William Asher ran for Marshal in the first town election but lost by 46 votes. That might have been due to a letter written to the editor of the *Nevada Journal* asking if Asher was a citizen of the town as his ranch was outside of town toward Grass Valley.

Asher sold the Phelps' Hotel in March 1854 to Samuel Green and Simeon Hussey. Plans were being made to erect a new brick building on the site when Green died unexpectedly of typhoid fever on April 19. Hussey leased the hotel in May to Samuel Hervey and Andrew R. Jenkins. The hotel was repaired and refurbished by them and opened a short time later under the name of the Metropolis Hotel.

In September of 1854 David Aldrich purchased the now pop-

The Phelps' Hotel after its removal to the north side of Deer Creek. (Drawing by David Allan Comstock from his book *Brides of the Gold Rush*.)

ular Metropolis Hotel from Simeon Hussey.[7] Aldrich reopened the hotel on November 3rd after improving it by "elevating the second story of the building," and enlarging and refurnishing to make it a desirable boarding house for families and popular with out-of-town guests. The California Stage company and the Red Dog Stage Line each opened an office at the hotel before the end of the year, with William S. McRoberts as agent for both companies. Soon all the other stage companies would follow their lead with stops at the hotel.

In January of 1856 David W. Aldrich retired and Mrs. I. Brooks from Sacramento was hired to manage the hotel. Six months later Aldrich and his wife Jennie sold the hotel property to Peter V. Skillman for $5,000, excluding the furnishings of the hotel.[8] Skillman was among the twenty men who built "fire-proofs" in 1855, bringing the number of brick buildings in Nevada City to 32 by an 1856 count.

Hussey either held a note when he sold the hotel to Aldrich or Aldrich never paid him the full amount, because in May 1856 there was a notice for a sheriff's sale to be held for the lot on which the Metropolis Hotel stood to satisfy a judgment by R. F. McConn against Hussey for $4,446. If Aldrich defaulted on his payment to Hussey then Hussey would have been deemed the owner and responsible for taxes and outstanding debts.

Most of Nevada City was destroyed by fire on July 19, 1856, including the Metropolis Hotel and its furnishings (a loss of $9,000) as well as his and Skillman's brick building, erected in 1855. Several of the fire-proofs were lost due to explosions caused by "powder" blowing up, a hazard for every mining town.

With this disaster many people lost their homes, businesses, money-on-hand and in the banks that burned, everything they had of value except their lives and the clothes on their backs. Most of the early pioneers who were still living in Nevada at the time of the fire had been burned out at least once or twice previously.

As a result Hussey would also lose his store and house; the property would be sold at a sheriff's sale before the year was out. Maybe it's bad luck to change the name of a hotel, similar to the long-held belief for changing the name of a boat.

4. Bricks and the Bicknell Block

THERE WERE THREE early brickyards just outside Nevada in the early days, and two were in operation by 1854. One was known to have three kilns by that date and was adding two more in order to increase the brick production. The other brick yard had two kilns and was kept busy with the constant influx of people to the area. Because bricks were in demand for construction in building wells, chimneys, fireplaces, as well as houses and stores, the brickyard dealers tried their best to keep up with ever increasing population.

In 1853 there was a shortage of bricks, which postponed the erection of such buildings until the spring of 1854. The first source, the Nevada Brick Yard, was located at the head of Broad Street in 1851. The second was located on the north side of Red Dog road about 1½ miles east of Nevada City. This yard changed hands several times in the early years and some of the early known owners were William B. Yates, William Kittle and William O'Donnell. A third brickyard was in operation by 1857, located on Murchie Road and owned by Horatio G. Phillips and Co. This company had made a million bricks that year and was expecting to produce an additional million and a half. This would make it possible for bricks to become affordable "enabling all to build brick houses and stores almost as cheaply as wooden."[1]

Another brickyard was later operated on Gold Flat by Daniel O'Donnell, brother of William O'Donnell, who later moved to Grass Valley and opened a brickyard there.

The first brick building was erected in 1853 by Hamlet Davis on Broad Street, near the corner of Pine—it was the same year that the telegraph came to Nevada City. The next year several other brick buildings were built, and in 1855 the following men were known to have brick buildings already completed or that were under construction: Zeno P. Davis, A. W. Potter, Dr. John Lark, Mr. King, Edward Kelsey, John Yates and David Tallman, John Ramus, John Grier and Patrick Henry, Abraham and Peter Skillman, B. F. and Julius C. Dickerman, William Bullington and William Alban, Simeon Hussey and Artemas Rogers, John C. Abbot and Thomas Edwards, Henry and Moses Hirschman, Aaron and Moses Rosenheim, Horatio Phillips and Co., Matthew H. Funston, Bernhard Franz and Co., Miss Mary Miller, John Parker and Israel Ash, George A. Young, Stillman Thomas, and Dr. H. V. Bicknell.

In the 1850s it was not unusual to build brick structures in sets of two or more, using common walls between them; the owners shared the expense of construction. These walls were a foot or more thick. A group of buildings using common walls was known as a "block."[2]

It was in September 1855 that George A. Young started building a brick *fire-proof* store adjoining (on the east) the brick buildings erected by Stillman Thomas, Zeno P. Davis and Dr. H. V. Bicknell on Broad Street. The buildings were three-stories high and set on an elevated site that towered above the creek and could be seen upon entering town from any direction. This particular group of buildings became known as the Bicknell block

Dr. H. V. BICKNELL.
Eclectic Physician and Surgeon
Office on Broad Street. 2d Door above the Union Hotel.

HE is prepared with accommodations for those who wish to place themselves under his care. Dr. Bicknell is also a thorough read and practically skilled Dentist, and will perform the following operations on the Teeth to the satisfaction of all who may favor him with a call, viz :

Teeth plugged with pure gold,		$3 00
do	do	tin-foil,	2 00
do	do	silver cement,	2 00
Teeth extracted,			1 00
Inserted on pivot,			5 00
Cleaned, for from $1 to			3 00

His Tooth Powder is unequalled for curing the Scurvy and making the Teeth white.

Jan. 21, 1853.   39 3mos*

Advertisement that ran in the *Nevada Journal* in 1853 and 1854 before the Bicknell block was built after Dr. Bicknell the physician, surgeon and dentist. Thomas's store was on the left (next to the alley), Dr. Bicknell owned the double-block in the center, and Zeno P. Davis, the first gunsmith in Nevada City, owned the store on the right.

By March of 1856 there were thirty-two brick buildings, deemed fire-proofs, in Nevada, twenty of which were built during 1855. The buildings of Young, Davis and Bicknell were still in progress in late October of 1855 as reported by the newspaper. We can assume that some were completed that season before the winter weather came to halt construction. Those buildings which were in progress and not yet completed would have been completed in the spring of 1856. The names of Young, Davis and Bicknell were listed in the March article as having been erected in the "last season." [3]

"Bicknell's Block, Nevada 1856," published by J. E. Hamlin, Bookseller, Nevada, California. The building on the left, and the right-hand portion of Bicknell's Block were gutted, but the two in the center withstood the 1856 fire. Hamlin's own building at Broad and Pine streets also survived.

5. The Nevada City Fire of 1856

IN 1856 THE TOWN OF NEVADA was at the height of her prosperity. Businesses were flourishing, and the amount of merchandise and goods had never been more abundant to serve the booming mining town, its residents and miners for miles around. Nevada was the county seat of Nevada County and the largest trading center that was accessible to the residents of up-country towns and the many mining camps for supplies and everyday necessities.

The fire that started in the afternoon of July 19, 1856, at Hughes' blacksmith shop on Pine Street probably will be remembered as the worst disaster in Nevada City's history, not only for the large monetary loss suffered in that disaster, but for the loss of lives. At least ten people perished in the fire, and at the time it was suspected that the count was higher. There may have been people who arrived in town that day whom no one knew, so were not reported among the missing. Two bodies found were never identified and could have been men who were just passing through town that day.

Of the thirty-two (one source claims there were twenty-eight and another thirty)[4] supposedly fire-proof brick buildings, only six survived and four of those were found to be on fire after opening the doors. Two brick buildings remained untouched: those of Dr. Bicknell on Broad Street and of Dr. Lark on Main Street. The two brick buildings on either side of the Bicknell block that were destroyed belonged to George Young and Zeno Philosopher Davis.

Crowds of people gathered above the town on the hills, where hundreds stood helplessly as they watched the spreading flames quickly destroy their homes, churches, government buildings and businesses. They looked down upon the former town, uncomprehending, at the almost total destruction that lay before them. It is hard to imagine that in so short a duration—one hour, the newspapers reported—brought almost total destruction to the flourishing town and busy county seat. It destroyed every

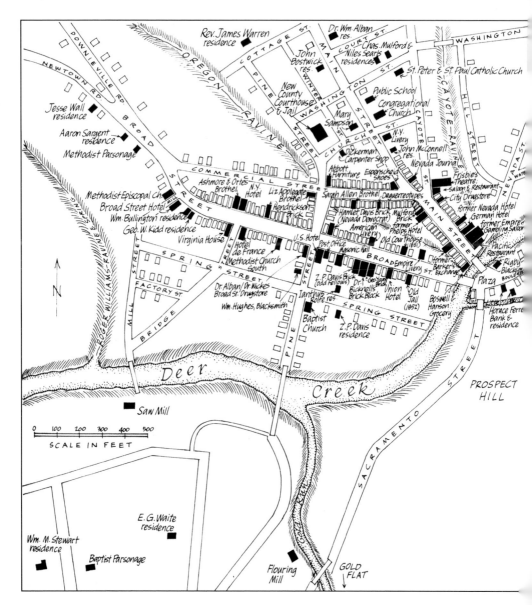

Nevada City as it appeared before the 1856 fire.
(Map by David Allan Comstock from *Brides of the Gold Rush*.)

wooden business structure in its path, and almost all of the private residences (except those above the business district, beyond the path of the fire). The most costly loss—excluding human lives—was the new court house, just completed at a cost to taxpayers of $60,000. The fire was driven by a strong westerly wind that quickly spread the blaze from roof to roof and blew embers from block to block until all that was left were piles of ashes and heaps of bricks.

Hotels lost in the fire were the Metropolis, United States, Broad Street, Yankee Blade, Union, Oriental, New York, Hotel de Paris, German, Virginia House, American, African, Pacific restaurant and hotel, and the Ross restaurant and boarding house. There were other boarding houses, both private and public, and other saloons and businesses with rooms above that contained living quarters that were lost in the fire. The 1856 fire was said to cost a staggering $1,500,000. (The loss would be equal to approximately $39,800,000 in 2010 dollars.)[5] Lives were changed forever for some, and for others it would not be the last time that they would witness the destruction of Nevada.

Kindness and courage always surface during and after a tragedy. A relief committee was quickly formed, and money came pouring in from nearby towns as well as from Sacramento, Iowa Hill, Forest City, Downieville and San Francisco. Among private donations the Rowe and Co. Circus benefit brought in $800. Those few residents whose dwellings were outside of the fire's path threw open their doors to the large numbers of destitute, some providing not only shelter but any funds and services they could give to the less fortunate. The *Nevada Journal,* in the first newspaper edition published after the fire reported: "The fire could not have originated in a more favorable place to destroy the entire town."

Below is the full account, written either by Edwin G. Waite (holding the office of state senator from Nevada County) or Aaron A. Sargent (holding the office of district attorney) or possibly one of the partners of Brown and Co.—Nat P. Brown, J. P. Skelton, Addison C. Niles or H. M. Fuller—who witnessed and participated in fighting the fire. The *Journal* lost its own building, with equipment, presses and all the back issues of the newspaper, as well as a member of their own staff. No writer of today could give a more heart-felt description of the disastrous event, or capture the eloquence and sorrow of the tragedy of that day with greater skill than whoever penned the story that appeared in the *Nevada Journal*:

Full History of the Destruction of Nevada
by fire, on the 19th of July.

It becomes us as eye-witnesses and sufferers in the late awful conflagration of or rich and thriving city, and as chroniclers of the events of passing time, to employ the first cool breath, after shaking from ourselves the cinders, the ashes, and the dust of our devoted home, in relating the story how Nevada vanished, in one short hour, in clouds of smoke and a whirlwind of fire.

That morning sun rose as bright on the 19th of July, on the fairest city of the mountains, as was his wont. Life swarmed in our streets, as if in the sealed book of fate, was not written DELENDA EST NEVADA. The joyous sun of the morning, set, a bloodshot eye, looking through volumes of smoke upon acres of blackened ruins.

At about 1 o'clock P.M. [The *Nevada Democrat* said between 3 and 4 pm], the startling cry of FIRE! hurried men from their stores and dwellings into the streets, and awoke hundreds from reveries of prosperity and happiness, to the certain realities of poverty and want. The fire broke out in Hughes' blacksmith shop, in the rear of Dr. Alban's brick, on Pine Street, between Broad and Spring. The wind blowing smartly from the west at the time, quickly communicated the flames across the street to the U.S. Hotel. The streets about the corners of Broad and Pine were immediately filled with human beings anxious and willing to risk even life to stay the destroyer; but the rapid progress of the flames, soon demonstrated that no earthly power was able to conquer the fiery element.

We have witnessed the indomitable will, activity, daring and skill of our citizens heretofore, in combating the flames, and better men any place may be challenged to produce. But the veterans of former conflicts, read in the increasing pyramid of fire, a conqueror, against whom it were mockery to contend, and the boldest stood aghast, or fled before the angry march of the swift and inexorable invader.

The fire could not have originated in a more favorable place to destroy the entire town. Hughes' blacksmith shop was connected with a long row of wooden building, occupying all that business portion of territory bounded by Broad, Pine and Spring streets. One brick, Dr. Alban's alone offered an obstacle to the flames in this quarter of the city. The wind, driving the flames in the direction of the U.S. Hotel, insured the demolition of the numerous wooden buildings, between Broad and Spring streets, from Pine to the bridge. The southwesterly side of Broad street, could not well be in a blaze, without commanding with a westerly wind, the entire business and valuable portion of the city, scattering brands in thick profusion far and near, until the whole combustible material of which the town was principally built, burst into sheets of flame and convolving clouds of inky blackness. It was evident from the first, that every wooden building in the heart of the city must be swept away. The only hope remained in the reputed fire-proof bricks, of which there were twenty-eight in number, and a few cellars and vaults, distributed here and there over the fated district. Hundreds of thousands of dollars in goods, poured into the bricks in the few moments allowed for removal. The doors and windows of these were shut and barred in the greatest haste, and the owners fled before the hot pursuit, joined the crowds of fugitives, unwillingly leaving all to be destroyed with fervent heat, and watched how well their costly buildings, salamander like, would stand the fiery ordeal.

Collected in crowds upon the hills, about an ocean of flame, were hundreds of the houseless and homeless, appalled by the scene before them, and the thoughts of the calamity which had befallen them. Billows of liquid flame dashed against the walls of brick, and swallowed them ever and anon from sight. The roaring, the crackling, the blazing faggots shot heavenward, the sooty pavilion of cloud that overhung all, and the intense anxiety of the many whose eyes were fixed upon the masonry that enclosed their all, hoping, doubting and fearing, make it a scene sufficiently grand and terrible. But when the unbidden news passed from mouth to mouth, that human beings, citizens and friends, the estimable and the good, were shut up within hot

23

walls, in the midst of the conflagration, and the solid masonry had not stood the test, how agonizing was the hour! Many a fervent unuttered prayer sought the throne of the Eternal at that trying moment. The testing hour of friendship, love, and humanity had come, and the trying altar was a burning city.

Four well known and valued citizens were confined In the brick buildings, erected by Hamlet Davis, on Broad street, known as the pioneer of its kind in Nevada. A large quantity of power blew up at about half past six o'clock, leveling the walls to the ground, and extinguishing the last hope, for the unfortunate victims. Thus perished A. J. Hagan, Jay Johnson, S. W. Fletcher and Wm. B. Pearson.

The fine brick of Hendrickson also blew up burying its owner [Peter Hendrickson] in the ruins. The equally fine structures of [Grier] and Skillman, on Main st. shared the same fate. The walls of the building of Rogers Hamilton & Co. would likewise have been demolished from the same cause, but from the timely foresight of Rogers in having the powder removed.

The walls of the three story brick of Abbott & Edwards on Commercial street fell from the great heat within and their own weight. These are the only brick buildings, the walls of which are hopelessly injured, through out of twenty-eight supposed fire proof buildings, but six escaped unburnt, and four of these were found, on opening the doors, to be either on fire, or to have been so. The fire proofs of Dr. Bicknell on Broad Street, and Dr. Lark on Main street, are the only ones that the destroyer did not enter. On opening the store of D. Crittenden on Main st. a carpet sack was found on fire, which was extinguished and the building and stock saved. A few shoes near the shutters in Espenscheid's brick, corner of Main and Commercial street, also ignited without doing any material damage. A cat in the building died of heat or suffocation. A most desperate fight was made to save the brick building of Dr. Alban, on the corner of Broad and Pine, near where the fire originated. After the fire and smoke had somewhat abated in the vicinity, J. E. Hamlin who occupies a portion of the building as Bookseller and Stationer, covering himself with a wet blanket made a rush to the front of the store, and by means of a part of a ladder lengthened with pieces of boards, entered a window in the upper story with the assistance of M. L. Marsh. The building was found to be on fire about the skylight, and the coals falling, had burned a hole through the floor, immediately below which, in the lower story was a large quantity of camphene. A bucket of water previously provided for emergency by Marsh and Hamlin, was thrown upon the burning floor by the latter, when he was obliged to retreat to the window nearly suffocated with smoke. Marsh now entered to his assistance. Mr. Thomas Whartenby about this time let loose his large reservoir and torrents of water came rushing through the burnt distract. A line was quickly formed; Mr. D. Belden, Frank Cleveland, Will N. Rabbitts and Jeremiah Tucker, mounted the ladder and fought like heroes till the fire was extinguished and a valuable building saved. Many others worked like tigers in this encounter whose names we have not learned. But for the courage, amounting to desperation, of Jimmy Hamlin and his coadjutors, Dr. Alban's building must have shared the doom of its mates.

A determined effort was made to save the new Court House, just completed at an expense to the county of near sixty thousand dollars. Some of those in the building, engaged in the hot warfare, barley escaped with their lives. The fire was burning on every side, and they were obliged to leave the Court House to its fate. The only hope of escape was in running the entire breadth of the burnt district, against the hot exhalations arising, and blown in their faces, to Deer Creek. Sheriff Wright, perfectly exhausted, was brought to a place of safety by Geo. Lewis, a prisoner, who had been let out of his cell, with the other prisoners, and who fought manfully to defend the property of the public, while a hope of its salvation remained. Lewis was admitted to bail in the sum of twenty thousand dollars, and is now at liberty.

By seven o'clock in the evening, the proud city, that a few hours before asked no favors from any, was blown to the winds in dust and ashes, leaving a blackened and smoking site where Nevada was, and was to rise again, like the fabled bird, from the ashes.

Such a complete annihilation of a city has never yet been witnessed, even in California, a land of fires. Every Church,

Hotel, Banking House, Printing Office, Store, the Post Office, County Records, Court House—in fact every thing but six brick buildings and their contents and a few cellars and vaults, containing a small quantity of goods, are among the things that were.

It is conceded, it was one of the most rapid fires, and the hottest, ever witnessed in the State. Safes were destroyed by the dozens, and others more or less injured. The air was oppressively hot on the hills across Deer Creek, at a distance of three hundred yards to the windward of the fire.

Though the labor and fruits of years are swept away, the acres of blackened earth mark the site of a town destroyed, and though houseless and homeless are hundred of our citizens, and comparatively penniless too, their stout hearts to not despair. They are made of sterner stuff. Not one among the sufferers, but has resolution and courage enough to lead a forlorn hope in a desperate conflict. The rebuffs of fortune only sharpen their determination like fighting bees in time of swarming. With such a population there is no such word as fail.

Nevada is rising again and the ashes of the old city will act as guano to the growth of the new. She is bound to sit among the hills again in greater beauty and opulence than ever. Iron railway bands shall bind her to the great metropolis of the Pacific, and the Nevada Journal shall yet be printed by steam. Does anyone doubt it? Let him look at the laborer among the smoke and heat, scraping always the coals and embers, and cooling a foundation for another structure, scared ere the flames have ceased to rage in another part of the city. Let him behold two hundred houses suddenly arise, as if called out of nothing by the waving of a magician's wand, and still see light and cheerful hearts, and hear the universal, everywhere, industrial, hum, click, clatter and rumble, and believe with a living faith.

Great as was the loss of property, it would be we recall the dead to the land of the living.

WM. B. PEARSON, was a printer in the Democrat office, a gentleman of unsullied character, unassuming in his manner, and well respected.

S. W. FLETCHER, formerly District Attorney of the County, was a young gentleman of great amiability and simplicity of character, noble, generous, and kind in all his impulses, a truer or firmer friend never breathed.

JAY JOHNSON, our former County Surveyor, was all heart and soul. A selfish thought he never cherished. He lived and died no man's enemy, leaving a blank that none can easily fill.

A. J. HAGAN was a banker, of integrity, full of life, hope and promise, of warm impulses and attachments. He has left numerous relatives and friends in this State, and elsewhere, to mourn his untimely fate.

PETER HENDRICKSON, was perhaps the most energetic and successful merchant in the city. As a business man he had few equals. From a few dollars, he rapidly accumulated a fortune among us, and friends as well.

JOHN YATES, of the firm of Yates & Tallman, perished in his brick building on Commercial street. He was an estimable man and citizen.

The remains of the six whose names we have mentioned, have been found, recognized and buried. Besides these, were found the remains of a man in Kelsey's brick on Commercial street, and the calcined bones of a human being, where the Polka stood, on Broad street. Add to these Messr's [William] Wilson and Thomas who were so badly burned in the fire, they died soon after, and we have ten persons who lost their lives by the conflagration of the 19th ult.

Several persons were severely scorched. Mr. Wm. Anderson, Editor of the Democrat, with his brother-in-law, George A. Young, came near perishing in the flames. Both were badly burned. The life of the former has been despaired of, but both, we are happy to state, are rapidly recovering.

Many remarkable incidents of the fire are related.

T. [E.] Beans, Esq., Deputy County Clerk, jumped from the second story of the pioneer brick, after calling upon Fletcher to follow him, and escaped unhurt through the flames.

The escape of Mrs. Frisbie, from the upper story of the building adjoining and connected with the Journal office, was almost providential. In the hurry, the doors in front were shut, all the shutters being previously closed. Perfectly self possessed, finding it impossible to get out in front, she felt her way in the dark through halls and rooms to the rear of the building, and tried to unbar the shutters of two windows that would not yield. Some time before, thinking of such an emergency, she had taught herself the mysteries of opening and shutting the iron fastenings of the building, and the bars of one shutter not working easily, she took the precaution of greasing them. These alone yielded to her efforts, and she escaped by a ladder. But first, before leaving, she examined a dozen bed rooms to see that none was left to perish. Thus did womanly instincts triumph over danger to self?

A cat was discovered on breaking into the vault of C. [Charlie] W. Mulford, Banker, twenty hours after the fire was over, alive but singed, yet fully realizing the expression, "a singed cat is better than she looks."

A list of sufferers and losses appeared in the same issue and in the next as well.

Natural causes and accidents were not the only threat to the early mining towns. Just two weeks after the Nevada City fire, a man by the name of Pat Gallagher was charged with attempting to burn down the town of North San Juan. He had been caught striking a match to light some shavings in the rear of Ned Pratt's store. It was leaned that Gallagher was hired by another party to set the fire, but someone had been alerted and Gallagher was apprehended before the fire had a chance to catch.

Golden Nuggets

- The first sign hung up after the fire was that of H. & M. Hirschman, Cigar Dealers.

- A few of the businesspeople had been hurt by fire several times. Early pioneer Lyman P. Frisbie had been burned out for a total of *seven* times and still he decided to stay and rebuild after the 1856 fire. The Frisbie Theatre was said to have been one of the most elegant in the state and could accommodate 800 persons.

6. The First Brick Hotel

NEVADA CITY'S FIRST brick hotel in opened its doors a month after the fire on Wednesday, August 20, 1856, under the management of Henry H. Pearson and Joseph Healey, the previous proprietors of the United States Hotel.[1] They had announced that the new hotel would open its doors on Monday, August 18, but apparently it wasn't quite ready on that date.[2]

> ### National Exchange,
> BICKNELL'S BLOCK, BROAD ST.
> THE ABOVE HOTEL WILL BE OPENED
> On Monday, August 18th,

The United States Hotel had been closed the previous March, having been leased by Thomas W. Coburn and Andrew R. Jenkins. Coburn had filed a petition to the court to be discharged from debts as an insolvent debtor. Pearson and Healey reopened the United States Hotel on Broad Street in late March, after having renovated and refitted the premises, and was operated by them for only four months before the July 19th fire destroyed it.

Having leased the "fire proof brick block" owned by Dr. Bicknell, the new proprietors could boast that the building had withstood the 1856 fire and that they were confident of making the National Exchange Hotel one of the most desirable hotels in the mountains. The rooms were advertised to be airy and well furnished with all new furniture, and from the balconies there was a splendid view of the surrounding country.

George and Charles Keeney

In May of 1856 local merchant George Keeney had run for Nevada City trustee on the Citizens ticket against his neighbor, Tallman H. Rolfe, the *Nevada Democrat* editor.[3] The Democratic candidates running for office that year won every position in the local election.

In addition to being a merchant, George Keeney was a tinsmith, and in August of 1856 he had begun erection of a one-story brick building at 14 Main Street for his hardware and tin business.[4] George Keeney acquired the Bicknell block at a sheriff's auction held on the courthouse steps on December 20, 1856. The sale of the property had been advertised in the local newspaper for the required period to give the owners the right of redemption if they chose and/or were able to do so. Sheriff William Butterfield sold the property after an Order to Sale was issued by Judge Niles Searls from an action brought by Keeney against Bicknell and Stillman Thomas in the amount of $7,080, and a second suit for $3,336.40 owed by Bicknell. The total was $10,416.40, and proceeds from this sale were to apply to the judgment in favor of Keeney.

On February 25, 1857, a quit claim deed was signed and later recorded, transferring the property from Bicknell to Keeney for the sum of $100. Local historian and author David Comstock, when questioned about the judgments against Bicknell, surmised that "Every businessman in town (including Keeney) was hurt by the fire of July 19, and they scrambled to collect sums owed so they could rebuild and restock."[5] Dr. Bicknell was apparently not able to meet his obligations—perhaps a note was carried for the property and money was borrowed against it, or Bicknell may have borrowed money from Keeney. All county records at the county courthouse were lost in the fire, and unless the parties re-recorded them after that date, no public records have survived to search. Original deeds would have gone to the new buyer.

It is hard to comprehend the very substantial losses of the residents and businessmen as a result of the fire that may have included their homes, all personal belongings, businesses, all stock and cash in-hand and in the banks that burned.

Around the same time Keeney also had two empty buildings available in Nevada City, and he was advertising them for rent in June 1857. They had been recently rented out as a bakery and saloon. Keeney was a popular and respected businessman, and even though he had lost the election for city trustee the previous year, in September of 1857 he was appointed by the elected trustees to be an inspector for a special election for the proposition to "supply the city with water, and to protect the city against fires."[6]

There is no evidence that Keeney was ever an on-site manager of the hotel, even though he was the legal owner of the National Exchange building. On December 1, 1858, George Keeney sold the hotel property to his brother, Charles Carter Keeney, for $15,000. At the time of the sale Charles Keeney was a physician and surgeon in U.S. Army and lived at the army base at San Francisco. Dr. Charles Keeney may have purchased the hotel property as an investment. In 1862 he became medical inspector and was promoted to the rank of colonel on June 30, 1882. Coincidently, he died exactly one year later, on June 30 1883.

Golden Nuggets

- Along with his medical duties, Charles C. Keeney was one of the early weather observers at the Presidio in San Francisco, California from October 1858 through April 1860, then again in July of 1860.[7]

- Also running on the Democratic ticket in May of 1856 was candidate W. Henry Plumer, who ran against Stephen Venard for sheriff. Plumer carried the day, but there were rumors the election was rigged. Plumer later left Nevada City after killing two men, and was hanged in 1857 without trial by the controversial Montana Vigilantes for allegedly directing the activities of a criminal gang while serving as sheriff in that place.

- Venard was said to have been one of the most fearless lawmen in the Gold Rush and later worked for Wells Fargo, becoming a hero after a tracking down bandits who robbed a Wells Fargo Stagecoach near Nevada City. California Governor Frederick Low appointed Venard to his staff in 1866 with the rank of Lieutenant Colonel in the National Guard, and Wells Fargo presented him with a new gold-mounted Henry Rifle. In that same year he became deputy sheriff of the boom town of Meadow Lake, Nevada County. In 1871 Venard came back to Nevada City to serve as a police officer.

7. Nevada City's 1858 Fire

THE 1858 FIRE WAS another major calamity to Nevada City and her residents, and it is surprising that little has been written about it since that time. Again fire left the city of Nevada in ashes, almost destroying the entire town by consuming more than 200 buildings and houses. Fortunately the court house and all the churches were saved, with the one major loss of a public building, that being the Frisbee's Theatre.

On May 23 a fire broke out on Broad Street below the White Hall Stables. The fire was blamed on the carelessness of an "opium smoking Chinaman," Win Kee. It was reported by the newspaper that fire had visited that same building five or six times within two or three months.

The extent of the conflagration was blamed on the want of organized action and lack of effort during the first half hour after the onset of the fire. Except for the nonchalance of the crowd in the street, the town might have been saved. This fire's progress was slow and lacked the high winds of the unfortunate 1856 fire which had caused that fire to spread so rapidly. There were plenty of buckets available and an abundance of water in back of the Hotel de Paris to have put out this fire in a very short time if the effort had been made or someone had come upon the scene to take charge and call for action. It's hard to understand this lack of concern by the watching crowd when many of the townspeople had witnessed the town completely destroyed several times to one extent or another, and fewer than two years had passed since the July 1856 fire.

Aaron Sargent, Ed Wheaton and others fought the fire, and their efforts saved the New York Hotel, but actions by other level-headed men appeared to be few and far between.

Credit was given to Mrs. John A. Lancaster after the fire for her appeals to save the bridges at the foot of Broad and Main Streets.[1]

The May 28th edition of the *Nevada Journal* expressed the importance of erecting buildings made of brick in light of the

Diagram of the Burnt District.

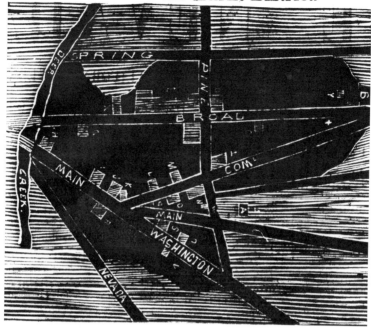

+—Fire Originated.
A —Court House.
B —Methodist Church.
C —Flagg & Riley's brick, occupied by R. Fininger.
D —Jesse Wall's, and the Alban brick building.
E —Harrington & Patterson's saloon; Lampe's barber shop; Democrat building; Caswell's, Hunt's, and Riley's bricks; Post office, and National Exchange.
F —Kidd & Knox's brick.
G —A. Sanford's brick feed store.
H —John Grier's and Davenport's.
I —Hirshman's, Rosenheims' and Hamilton's brick block.
J —Mulford's and Rosenthal's bricks.
K —Chas. W. Young's jewelry store
L —Keeny's hardware store.
M —Bailey Gatzert provision store.
N —Riley's, Abbott's and Kelsey's buildings.
O —Brick block, occupied by Tallman & Turner, Geo. O. Kilbourn, and D. & B. Lachman.
P —Espenschied & Coe's boot and shoe store.
R —Buildings occupied by Geo. Welch and Dr. Bailey.
S —Buildings occupied by Gregory & Wickes, and F. W. May & Co.
T —George O. Kilbourn's brick building, occupied by Cheap John.
U —Barton's brick blacksmith's shop.
V —Frisbie's brick store-house.
W—Dickerman's Carpenter shop and paper hanging establishment.
X —Union Hotel, wood.
Y —Mrs. Von Poellnitz' residence, and two small wooden buildings.

Nevada Democrat diagram of the 1858 burnt district, where fire burned almost the same area as in the 1856 and 1863 fires.

number of times that the town had been destroyed before. At that time there was still no fire department or dedicated facilities for fighting fires, but owners of property continued to construct buildings and houses of wood due to the lower cost. The *Journal's* editor claimed that the higher cost of building with brick was only slight and tried to appeal to the building owners' common sense:

> There has been property enough destroyed by fire in Nevada to build the entire town of brick and furnish a deluging torrent at every door. It is not absolutely necessary that all the buildings about to be erected should be fire-proof. A few brick walls to afford shelter to those who were fighting the flames the other day would have done wonders. Men cannot be expected to stand exposed to a fierce furnace, with nothing to shield them, and do much service. Brick fronts not fire proof would have saved rows of buildings on the other side of the street last Sunday from the flames and confined the destruction to moderate limits.

The thirty brick buildings in the town—as well as fire-proof cellars where large stocks of goods were stored—survived the fire, although there was some damage to brick mentioned in the loss claims. The only building of public note to be destroyed was Frisbie's Theatre.

Nevada Democrat editor Tallman Rolfe thanked the many townspeople who helped save his firm's building and equipment:

> We are under many obligations to Messrs. E. G. Waite, S. H. Chase, A. B. Paul, Geo. Hurst [sic], and a number of others, for their timely services, in assisting to remove the materials of our office at the time of the fire. But little hopes were at first entertained of saving the building, consequently every thing of value, except a press, was removed. We are also indebted to some forty or fifty other citizens, who worked for nearly an hour with unflagging energy to save the building. Notwithstanding the almost super-human exertions that were used, the building would probably have been consumed, but for the coolness and courage of Geo. Ferrend and Geo. I. Lammon, who, when the heat was the most intense, and the danger imminent, carried water to the front, and extinguished the fire which had caught the

blankets that were hanging over the gable. About this time, the burning buildings on the opposite side of Broad street fell in, and the critical time was over.

Golden Nuggets

- In January of 1858 a meeting was held at the National Hotel by citizens who desired to avenge their country's wrongs by enrolling for the Mormon War. Thomas Henry was chosen as Captain and James S. Curtis First Lieutenant.

- During the same month two routes between Grass Valley and Nevada City were surveyed by a company for the purpose of constructing a Plank and Turnpike Road between the two places. The road was deemed very much needed, and stock would be sold to finance the enterprise.[2]

- In April a new saloon was opened on Broad street on the street floor of the National Hotel. The Senate sported two Billiard tables, and the bar was supplied with "the choicest liquors to be had in the State and sold at only one-bit a glass." Thomas Holmes was the manager of the newest and largest saloon in Nevada City.

8. The Lancaster Brothers and the 1863 Fire

IN MID-SEPTEMBER 1858, George R. Lancaster leased the National Exchange Hotel, the hotel now having survived two major fires that had destroyed most all of the business district in each instance. George and his brother John were pioneer residents of Nevada County and Nevada City who came from the state of Maine. The three-story hotel now had all of the comforts and accommodations a traveler of the mid-nineteenth century might desire. It was enlarged and refurbished by Lancaster as soon as he took over the management, and he purchased new furnishings and beds that he "fitted up in a style that cannot be surpassed."[1]

The hotel's menu included game suppers, and Lancaster's corned beef dinner was said to be *pre-eminent*. Lancaster did his own pickling. He advertised that he took extra care to accommodate ladies and families—so as not to neglect gentlemen, the bar and billiard tables were open all night, "fitted with the choicest wines, liquors and cigars."

A livery stable was connected to the hotel to take care of guests' horses, carriages and wagons and provide the same for rent. All of the stages operating at the time, running in all directions from Nevada City, had their offices at the National Exchange. No doubt the hotel's reputation spread far and wide, for Lancaster was a popular landlord and citizen.

Lancaster left California in 1864 to go back to his home state of Maine, but returned to Nevada County in 1877 for a visit. He died in 1888 in Maine, his brother having died several years earlier at Oakland, California.

The Infamous Fire of 1863

It was the fire of 1863 that closed the doors of the National Hotel, and almost brought it down. Its walls were left standing, but it had been badly gutted and the losses were so major that the hotel was not able to operate until substantial repairs were made. The hotel had suffered so much damage that the *Nevada Daily Transcript* reported on November 13th that it was doubtful the National would reopen:

GOING TO REBUILD.—Mike Lewis arrived in town on Wednesday night, and is making preparations to put the fine building commonly called the Flagg building, on the corner of Broad and Pine, in complete repair, and in about the same shape as before. It is a good place for business. Capt. Kidd is going to put Hamlin's building, on the opposite corner, in repair also, without delay. The brick buildings in front of the Transcript office on Commercial street are to be put up again as soon as possible. The Odd Fellows will reconstruct their building, but, ***the prevailing opinion at present is, that the National Exchange hotel will never be resuscitated***.[2]

Before the fire, then owner Charles C. Keeney's tax assessment for the National Hotel and property was based on a valuation of $16,000, with the yearly tax coming to $371.20. The amount of damage to the National Hotel building and contents was the largest claimed for any structure burned in 1863. The building was insured for $10,000, and after the fire it was supposed that amount would just about cover the cost to bring the building back into operation. In addition to the major damage to the building itself, in the original list of losses printed in the *Transcript* lessees Samuel L. Hasey and E. B. Mayberry listed the loss of "hotel furniture, beds, &c." to be $15,000. Bartender Andrew R. Jenkins claimed a loss of $5,000 for billiard tables, liquors, bar fixtures, cigars, tobacco, etc. An additional loss in the amount of $5,000 was claimed by the hotel's boarders for clothing, jewelry and personal property—making a grand total of $35,000. [3]

The 1880 *History of Nevada County* explains the apparently distorted and seemingly small monetary loss of the 1863 fire (when compared to the much higher figure for the 1856 fire) in this fashion: "It must be remembered also that the class of buildings [in 1863] was far superior to those burned before, larger and constructed of better materials. Owing to the decline in values since 1856 and to the fact that the loss of merchandise was but slight in comparison to that in the former fire, the comparative smallness of the loss, $550,000, will be readily understood. All the hotels and restaurants, every church but the Baptist, the court house, nearly every business building and a large number of residences were burned."[4]

The condition of the National was not as bad as first reported. It was not able to serve as a hotel immediately after the fire or during the reconstruction period, but it was not a total loss either. The town was rebuilding rapidly and by the end of November much progress had been made. The townspeople were hoping for continued good weather in order to finish before conditions changed. "Our great want is a hotel. But the rivalry that is showing itself in that line will soon produce at least two good ones—better than the town ever had before."[5]

Broad Street.

G. E. Withington, 2 buildings, stock.	2,000
E. F. Bean, post office fixtures, &c.	1,500
City Hall, calaboose, etc.	500
W. C. Groves, shop, tools, &c.	2,000
H. W. Wendler, stock of furniture,	4,000
National Exchange Hotel furniture, beds, &c. Hasey & Mayberry,	15,000
Loss of clothing, jewelry, &c. by the boarders,	5,000
National Exchange Hotel, building.	10,000
A. R. Jenkins, billiard tables, liquors, bar fixtures, cigars, tobacco, &c.	5,000
L. Chandler, hay, barley, building, &c,	3,000
H. Ernst, bookbinders tool, &c.	300
John Jenkins house and furniture,	2,000
Martin, house, &c.	500
Old Union Hotel,	300
A. R. Irish, carpenter's shop,	200
Drake, blacksmith shop, tools, &c.	600
A Sanford, building, feed, etc.	3,000
Odd Fellows' Hall, (ins. $7,500)	16,000
J. H. Helm, stable, carriages, etc.	5,000
Fisher & Lampe bath house, fixtures,	1,500
A. E. Head, house and furniture,	2,000
J. A. Cross, two stores,	2,000

Newspaper report of losses on Broad Street shows amounts related to the National Hotel.

The fire of 1863 burned five buildings fewer than the 1856 configuration. Men who knew how to turn a phrase penned the contemporary account in the *Daily Transcript* on Tuesday morning, November 10th:

>   ***Terrible Conflagration.***—Nevada is again in ashes! An alarm of fire was sounded at quarter to 12 o'clock on Sunday morning. The flames were found to originate in the rear of the Bed Rock Saloon, on the south side of Broad street, about six or seven doors above Pine. Pennsylvania No. 2's were promptly on the ground, but from some unaccountable cause there was little pressure to the water. The other fire companies were out in time, but the fire spread rapidly. It crossed Broad street in a few minutes and spread in every direction. At 5 ¼ P.M., the whole business portion of the town was in ashes, including the Court House, Engine Houses, and everything but the few fire-proof buildings that withstood the fire. The loss is terrible, footing up $500,000. Many have lost all they have. Luckily but few families have been un-housed, the residences being mostly built outside on the hills. All hotels and restaurants in the city are destroyed, and all the churches except the Baptist. The plank streets are generally ruined; Fifteen thousand dollars would not make them good. The Court House is burnt, but the records in all the County offices and all the funds are safe. The Court House might have been easily saved, if but two sections of hose could have been obtained, but they were not to be had. Many of the buildings saved owe their existence to the exertions of individuals. Probably the buildings about the corner of Commercial and Pine were so saved, as well as Crawford's, Dr. Hunt's, Spence's and other brick structures. The flames were also prevented from spreading to the residences on the hills by the hard work.

>   It seems strange that a town, as well defended against fires, as perhaps, any in the world, should have met such a fate. The reservoirs were full, and there was an abundance of water, but with one hundred and fifty feet at least perpendicular pressure the hose pipes would not throw water to the top of the buildings during the first three hours of the fire. Towards the last, the water worked better, but too late. Various causes have been assigned for this singular state

of things. Some allege that a gate to the pipes was closed. The matter needs investigation. As far as the South Yuba Canal Company is concerned, they saved all their water for the town and had their reservoirs full at the time during the fire.

We give another column a list of losses as near as we can obtain them in the distracted state of affairs. There is little despondence and the people are full of life and if the fine weather continues, the burnt district will soon present a different appearance.

A list of losses appeared in several columns of the same issue and was updated for several days thereafter, with the following weeks giving news of both good and bad relating to the fire.[6]

The residents, firemen and officials were enraged, knowing that the Nevada Water Works was in good working order prior to the fire but there was a stoppage somewhere and someone was responsible for it. There was an official investigation by the city and county and affidavits were taken. It was stated over and over that there was a problem with the water almost the entire time of the fire where only a "miserable stream of not more than thirty feet could be thrown at the flames."[7] It became apparent from the investigation that the water was shut off, at either the head of the works or at the juncture of Broad street and Hixson Hill, or possibly at both places.

One thing was certain: the reservoirs were full on the morning of the fire, but water did not flow through the pipes of the water works, and because of that the town was destroyed. Accusations were made about who was responsible and names were named.

Corrected lists of the losses continued to appear after the fire as many people disputed the accuracy of their losses as reported, some claiming their losses were much higher than what was reported in the paper. The *Transcript's* editor noted that many of the disputed claims seemed to be substantially higher than the dollar amounts listed in the assessor's records.

At a meeting of Nevada Hose Co. No. 1 on January 11, 1864, the members brought forth several resolutions. The one below was directed at the water company, claiming that the fire company did not have the privilege of access to the water gate that controlled the flow into the water pipes:

> *Resolved,* That in our opinion, the Nevada fire department have had, or could have had ample control of the water works to insure the city against disaster, and the citizens who maintain the department should not be made to suffer for the neglect or refusal of the department to avail themselves of such privileges grated them. Be it understood that we do not excuse the proprietor of the works in closing gates or otherwise interfering with the free flow of water through the pipes.[8]

Golden Nuggets

- On November 17th the *Transcript* reported that winds and rain had caused the front and rear walls of the court house to come down during the night. The other two walls did not look like they were in very good shape and should probably be taken down. A week later City Marshal William H. Davidson, using a chain-gang from the county jail, went prospecting through the ruins of the court house, hoping to unearth the bell. They found what remained of it—the clapper and yoke—the rest having melted in the fire.[9]

- After the fire many of the firemen of the three volunteer fire companies threatened to quit due to remarks that many firemen were not fighting the fire but trying to save their own homes. It was not the fault of the firemen that there was very little or no water available when they hooked up the fire hoses to the pipes. When the firemen found there was no water available some left to try and save their own property.

Major Fires in Nevada County Through 1863

Township	Date	Loss in 1850 dollars	Loss in today's dollars*
Nevada	March 11, 1851	500,000	14,500,000
Grass Valley	Sept. 1852	unknown	---------------
Nevada	Sept. 12, 1852	25,000	716,000
Rough & Ready	June 28, 1853	59,700	171,000,000
Nevada	Nov. 28, 1854	6,000	158,000
Nevada	Feb. 20, 1855	40,000	1,540,000
Grass Valley	Sept. 13, 1855	400,000	102,000,000
Nevada	July 19, 1856	1,500,000	391,000,000
Nevada	May 23, 1858	207,000	5,570,000
Rough & Ready	July 8, 1859	67,850	1,810,000
Grass Valley	Aug. 9, 1860	40,000	1,060,000
Grass Valley	June 11, 1862	24,000	520,000
Grass Valley	Aug. 15, 1862	40,000	800,000
Nevada	Nov. 8, 1863	500,000	8,810,000

Losses in today's dollars from www.measuringworth.com using 2009 as a comparison to show the measure of today's purchasing power.

9. National Exchange Hotel Company

A CORPORATION WAS FORMED on November 26, 1863, for the purpose of constructing and maintaining a hotel on Broad Street in the City of Nevada under the name of the National Exchange Hotel company, and the amount of capital stock of the corporation was $20,000 divided into 200 shares. The original terms of the corporation stated that the corporation would exist for 50 years and be managed by a board composed of three trustees. The following men were named on the original incorporation to act as trustees for the first three months until successors were elected: George W. Kidd, James Monroe and John Cashin. Signing the incorporation were John Cashin, Charles Chandler and Joshua N. Turner

Photo taken of lower Broad Street in 1857. National Hotel is building at left.

The first hotel to open its doors after the fire was the New York Hotel on December 21. Due to the season the weather was inclement. By Christmas day the Union Hotel on Main Street had its roof completed; the *Transcript* noted that the "hotel on Broad Street did not and if there were a few days of tolerable weather the roof to that hotel would be on."[1] The brick work on the National was almost finished and if the expected storm was not too severe, its roof could be completed by the first of January.

The National and the Union now would be the largest hotels in Nevada City, and the Union would be the National's number one competitor for decades to come. The newspaper claimed the structures would be "two of the best hotel buildings outside of San Francisco."[2] The race was on to open their doors to the public. Although the hotel was not ready for occupancy the hotel restaurant opened its doors the first week in 1864.

Throughout January there were meetings, long editorials printed in the newspapers and resolutions put forth to deal with the water question. This issue was of utmost importance to the townspeople and business leaders. The town was not lacking in organized fire companies, but rather a dependable and available source of water with which to fight the fire. If the water system had functioned as expected, it might have prevented the town from being destroyed.

Competition between the two hotels continued throughout January and near the month's end the front of the Union was finished and the inside work continued. In the meantime, the National was also progressing, and before the end of the month new iron shutters were almost finished to make it *fire proof.*

It was nearly the end of February—the 19th—when the doors to the Union Hotel were opened to the public under the management of Charles F. Miller (formerly of the National Exchange Restaurant at Broad and Pine streets), although the rooms of the hotel were not yet ready for occupancy. It was announced by Lancaster & Company that there would be a grand ball at the "mammoth" Union Hotel on Main Street on Washington's Birthday, February 22, and predicted it would be the grandest affair to take place in a mountain town of California. There were over 1,000 invitations sent out. Apparently Lancaster had only rented the ballroom and dining rooms, which were available for individuals and organizations to rent for parties and large social affairs at the Union.

On February 20, 1864, a notice was placed in the *Transcript* announcing that the stockholders of the National Exchange Hotel Company would be meeting at the office recently occupied by Addison C. Niles in the Kidd building for the transaction of the corporation's business. As a result of that meeting officers were elected for the next year: Secretary, Charles C. Leavitt; Treasurer, George W. Kidd; trustees elected were John Cashin, James Monroe and H. C. Miller.

It was claimed that the nearly completed National's appearance was "a hundred percent better than before the fire." Things were really progressing, but the one question going around town the first week of February was: who were to be the new proprietors of the Union and National hotels?

By the first week in March an announcement was made that John A. Lancaster and Samuel Hasey, both with a great deal of hotel experience, had leased the National and that it would open by the end of the month. Samuel Hasey may have been related to the Lancaster brothers, whose brother-in-law Andrew Hasey had been a resident of Nevada City before being nearly killed in 1860 by Paiute Indians at Pyramid Lake.

A few days later Lancaster and Hasey left for San Francisco

Blank or used National Exchange Hotel Stock Certificate. Stock certificates like this sell for hundreds of dollars on e-Bay and other auction sites.

to purchase furniture to have it shipped to the hotel. Abram B. Carley and Alden W. Potter would operate the new saloon and billiard parlor and a barber shop on the ground level, connected by a stairway to the hotel upstairs. (Potter was from Massachusetts and in 1870 was living with Frank Potter, two years younger and also born in Massachusetts.) The barber shop would later become the National Exchange Hotel "Shaving and Bath Saloon."

The offices of the California Stage Company were to be moved into the National Exchange Hotel and would be operating when it opened—the other stage companies soon would follow.

Because the U.S. Civil War was underway in 1864, Hasey and John A. Lancaster were presented with a gift of a large American Flag by John's brother George, to be hung from a flag pole 140 feet high in front of the hotel. George Lancaster, a former proprietor of the hotel, had recently visited Nevada City and his old home. When the flag pole, dubbed a "Liberty Pole," was erected on April first, the hotel managers were surprised at the large turnout for the event, more persons than they thought were left in town. Added to the top of the flag pole a few days later was a top mast of a "mackerel bird" to indicate which way the wind blew, and soon the magnificent new flag was raised by Sarah Lancaster, wife of George.

The National Hotel officially opened to the public on Monday, April 4, 1864.[3] Later that month it was announced that Ira A. Eaton and "Uncle Ike" Williamson had leased the Union hotel. Uncle Ike was well known in the community and Eaton had come to Nevada City from Marysville. The Union Hotel opened to the public on April 18 and advertised it had " . . . one hundred light and airy rooms, not a dark room in the house." It also had a dining room, bar and billiard room, large ball room and, like most hotels of the day, offered room and board for the local townspeople.

By the end of April there was little evidence left to testify to the disastrous fire of the previous November. A few vacant lots here and there, but most houses had been replaced by more substantial structures and the city presented a better appearance than before the fire—although the cost had been great.

Golden Nuggets

- In February 1865 it was learned from newspaper accounts that early resident and ex-marshal Henry Plumer, formerly of Nevada City, was hanged at Bannack City, Montana on January 10, 1865 by a vigilance committee. The committee was organized from all over the territory and thirteen persons had been hanged by them. "No man stands higher in the estimation of the community than Henry Plummer [sic]." *Sacramento Union*, May 1863

- A large ornate lamp was made for the National Hotel with the tin work done by Charles Tewksbury in Nevada City at George E. Withington's shop. It was reported to be magnificent.

- In 1865 the hotel prospered, and the town's increased growth required additional rooms. In January the National Hotel Company had purchased a vacant lot adjoining the hotel. That lot had been purchased by the Odd Fellows in 1861 to build a hall that was destroyed in the 1863 fire. By mid-1866 the National Hotel Company had decided to build a large three-story brick addition on it that would measure 40 feet on Broad Street and be 100 feet deep. The bottom floor would contain store rooms and the upper stories would add fifty additional guest rooms, making it the largest hotel outside of San Francisco. The hotel would then have a 120-foot frontage on Broad Street.

- By 1867 the stagecoaches of the Colfax, Alpha, Washington, Omega, Moore's, Woolsey's and Orleans Flat, Red Dog and North San Juan stage lines had offices at the National, which was open all night. The departures would be announced from the lobby for the four- and six-horse stages. Virginia City, Nevada, was "only 18 hours by stage from Nevada City." It was more convenient to stay at the National than find a room elsewhere. The stage arrival lists printed daily in the

Transcript included hundreds of names. Passenger trains on the partially completed Central Pacific Railroad line connected at Cisco (going east) and at Colfax (going west).

• The business district had grown and shifted slightly away from Main and Commercial streets, and the location of the National Hotel on Broad street had become more the center of town. The New Year saw a large number of buildings and houses being erected or improved in Nevada City, and the sounds of saws and hammers, as well as the unloading of building materials—both brick and lumber—could be heard in every part of the city. Likewise, the streets and sidewalks were being rebuilt or extended to include every part of town.

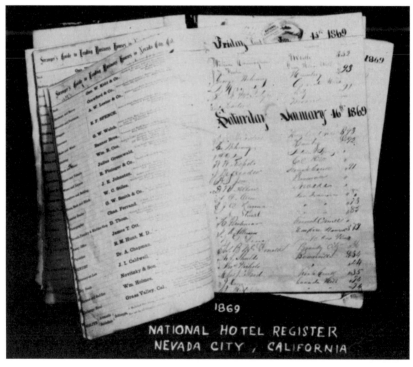

Old postcard photo of 1869 National Hotel register.

NATIONAL EXCHANGE HOTEL.

Broad Street, Nevada City, California.

LANCASTER & HASEY, Proprietor.

October 28, 1866.

Mark Twain San Franc		W Allport Red Dog	
W E F Kraus	do	V Curran Little York	
W F Hitchcock	do	J C Boynton R & Ready	
A K Lincoln	do	G Street Sacramento	
M Brown Rush Creek		F Slawek	do
F Brown	do	H Dunden Unionville	
J Barber Woll Creek		P Cordin Moores	
C R Clark Grass Valley		G A Townsend Brush C	
H C Wormwood	do	J Shaw	do
L B Clark	do	H Irwin Grizzly Canon	
D A Mitchell Nevada		Col Alby San Juan	
H A Ashburn	do	C Haymond Plumas Co	
J Overdorff	do	J H Bumbardner San Jo	
F Willis	do	J F McCourtney Bear Ri	
W Holbrook	do	J McNally Nevada	
J A Swarts	do	J L Cooper Yuba Bridge	
S B Davenport	do	S Baker Scott Flat	

The National Exchange Hotel was where the stage arrived and this is why some writers have claimed that Mark Twain stayed at the National. However, this 1866 newspaper arrival list does not offer proof of where Mark Twain stayed—in fact, It is said Twain roomed at the New York Hotel because it was across the street from the Nevada Theatre and convenient to where he lectured. The Nevada City newspaper did not mention where he resided, and current owner Tom Coleman does not have the register for 1866.

10. The Sunday Laws

WHILE SUNDAY LAWS were probably kept in most towns and cities in America at the time of the discovery of gold in California, the flood of would-be miners did not observe these customs. California was a part of Mexico in 1848, and the thousands of migrants from other countries and cultures from around the world brought diversity to California that was like no other place in existence.

In September 1851 there was a movement by part of the townspeople in Nevada City—backed by the clergy and churches, and agreeable to the merchants—to close businesses on Broad Street to allow a sufficient amount of time to attend divine services on the Sabbath. They hoped by example to persuade the whole city to take up the idea and close all stores and amusements for the entire day. It was hoped that by this time California could settle into more regular habits and the reign of vice and crime might end.

Grass Valley shut down its Sunday trade in the summer of 1853, and a Sabbath closing law was enacted in Nevada City two years later. On June 1, 1858, a law went into effect to observe the "Christian Sabbath" throughout the state. Many free-thinking Californians felt the law was unconstitutional, regardless of the existence of similar laws and traditions in the rest of the country. Some felt it was too "oppressive to be tolerated," and they ignored the law. Over the next two decades the battle continued in both the courts and the press until it reached the California Supreme Court in 1881.

While many businessmen in Nevada County were happy to comply with closing their shops and stores on Sundays, those most likely to oppose such laws were the saloon owners. After Andrew R. Jenkins of the National Exchange Saloon violated the state's newest Sunday Law he was tried three times in October 1861 before being convicted and fined $40. He was not alone in disregarding the law. Violators would simply plead guilty and pay the fines. It was well known by customers that if the front doors to their favorite drinking establishments were closed, a side door would be open. Consequently, the saloons would be full on Sundays, as had been the custom in California since 1849.

There was a loophole in the law, and Jenkins took advantage of it by transferring ownership of the saloon to George Lancaster, proprietor of the National Hotel. Jenkins continued to manage the saloon, but the transfer of title enabled Jenkins to sell liquor on Sundays without violating the law, because hotel restaurants were exempt from Sunday closures.

In the 1870s, while the Sunday Law was generally enforced in California, the one notable exception was the City and County of San Francisco. The authorities there believed that the law was "inoperative because of its contradictions and hence do not attempt to enforce it."[1] Sacramento, on the other hand, was diligent about upholding the law and arresting violators.

The strongest arguments put forth against the Sunday Law

The Deer Creek suspension bridge (later called the Gault bridge for Nevada City Mayor Alexander Gault) connected Grass Valley with Nevada City via Pine Street. Sugar Loaf hill is seen in the background, almost devoid of trees.

were its inequity and the language of the law itself. The law stated that a "tavern" could be kept open on Sunday, and they held to Webster's definition of a tavern as "a place at which liquors are sold in small quantities to be drunk on the spot."[2]

In Nevada County most businesses observed the law but those who didn't were not deemed lawbreakers. The press called for the Supreme Court to decide on the meaning of the word "tavern" and to clarify the intent and actual meaning of the law. Many felt the law was unnecessary and interfered with the rights of citizens and conflicted with the U.S. Constitution and the Bill of Rights. The law also was said to be inequitable and exclusionary due to exemptions for certain professions, including doctors, barbers and liverymen.

On December 9, 1881, an organization called the Branch League of Freedom of Nevada County was organized. It adopted a resolution for saloons and other businesses to be kept open on Sundays. One purpose of the statewide movement was to assist in the defense of any parties arrested for violating the law. Most every businessman in town joined or supported the League of Freedom. On the first Sunday after the local league's formation

Early undated photo of the National. Poster on side of the hotel advertises a circus coming on August 18.

every saloon in Nevada City remained open, along with a few other businesses.

All of California waited expectantly for the outcome of a Supreme Court case being heard at San Jose. It was debated until finally a decision was reached in mid-March of 1882. Justice Thornton, who rendered the decision, held "that the law is not special in its character, but on the contrary it is uniform in its operation and that by it no privilege of immunity is granted, so as to bring it in conflict with the Constitution. To hold such enactments unconstitutional and void would, in my best judgment, impose an unwarrantable restriction on the legislative power."[3]

Justices Morrison, Myrick and McKee concurred with Thornton while Justices McKinstry and Ross dissented from the decision. The Republican party supported the decision and Democratic party opposed it, and each side used the issue as a platform plank in the coming election campaign.

The court's decision did not end the battle or change the sentiments of saloon owners and many other businessmen. The Sunday Law was both a temperance and religious issue, and its opponents contended that it was wrong to impose the narrow moral standards and Puritanical judgments of one segment of the population upon all the others.

In February 1873 John Lancaster announced that the bar of the National Hotel would close on Sundays. In June Lancaster left Nevada City and moved to Oakland to manage the Grand Central Hotel, and died in October at age 45. He was replaced at the National Exchange in Nevada City by James F. Carr (who had worked as a clerk in the hotel for many years) and N. C. Tully, a former Nevada City grocer.

During the next few years the hotel changed management several times. In September Richard B. Gentry, a former Nevada County sheriff, purchased the controlling interest and Carr became his partner. Less than a year later, in July 1874, Gentry became the sole owner after Carr retired and bought a farm. By year's end Gentry had put up the hotel for sale and sold it to Col. Alden H. Eddy, a successful miner who had come to the county in 1850. His son, Stanley A. Eddy, managed the hotel from August 1876 to August 1877 and again during the 1880s.

11. Abel and Caroline Mead Hanson

ON SEPTEMBER 1, 1877, Abel H. Hanson became the proprietor of the National Hotel. Hanson was an early pioneer who came to Nevada City when he was about 20 years old and became a prosperous merchant in Nevada City. In *Brown & Dallison's 1856 Directory of Nevada, Grass Valley and Rough and Ready,* published before the fire, Hanson and his partner, S. B. Boswell, were listed as grocers at 1 Main Street. Boswell and Hanson lost $5000 in the 1856 fire. They rebuilt after the fire and added a large hall, perhaps above the store. They lost that building in February 1857 when the Deer Creek dam broke and flooded Nevada City. In the summer the partners built a new store.

On January 24, 1859, Hanson married Caroline Mead, daughter of Charles and Helena Mead, in the Congregational Church in Nevada City. After a number of ventures in which he operated grocery stores with a series of partners, in 1865 Hanson leased Dr. Robert M. Hunt's building next to the National Hotel In March of 1870 Hanson started a "grocery war" by advertising in *The Daily Transcript* that he would not accept credit any longer—his was going to be a *For Cash Only* store. He reduced all the prices of groceries and provisions in his store and announced that the prices would be corrected every morning. The grocery war had been preceded by a clothing war that apparently caused a good deal of excitement and proved to be good marketing maneuver.

On June 30, 1878, Abel Hanson ceased to operate the National Hotel. After Hanson left the National, Charles E. Pearson became its proprietor until August 1881, when Stanley A. Eddy was again managing the hotel. It may have been Hanson's heavy business losses in the early years followed by a series of dull times that caused him to file as an insolvent debtor at the end of 1881. The sheriff was ordered to take possession of all of Hanson's assets. About this time the Hanson family moved from Nevada City to Grass Valley.

Even though Hanson was a long-time resident, active in politics and a popular businessman, he would later be overshadowed in local history by his wife Caroline after she wrote a letter to the editor of the *Grass Valley Union* newspaper in November of 1883, proposing that school children be asked to bring a stick of wood and a potato to school to donate to the needy.

Caroline Mead Hanson and the Ladies Relief Society are credited with founding Donation Day in Grass Valley. The Donation Day Parade became a tradition that has continued over the decades and still is observed by school children and businesses in Nevada County who donate canned goods or money to be used to feed local needy families. The fame of the original Grass Valley's Donation Day spread to other states and cities.

Few today recall that Caroline Hanson's husband, Abel Hanson, once ran the National Hotel, but thousands still talk about Caroline Mead Hanson each year as another Donation Day is celebrated.

An early Donation Day Parade in Nevada City.

Golden Nuggets

- In late October of 1870 John Lancaster had grown two pumpkins on one vine that totaled 210 pounds in weight. The pumpkins were put on display at the National Hotel and rumor had it that Lancaster's guests had a splendid prospect for pumpkin pie for the coming Thanksgiving.

- In May of 1875 Mrs. Belle Chamberlain gave séances in room No. 15 of the National Hotel to "liberal minded ladies and gentlemen," and could accommodate about 25 persons. She laid hands on the sick and accepted free gifts as her reward.

- On January 19, 1882, a rope-walker stretched a line from the window of a third story of the National Hotel to the roof of the Empire Stable across Broad street. The performances were free and well-attended, but the "Professor" took up collections of coins between sets and he was said to be very funny, keeping the crowd in good humor.

- A funeral service was held at the National Hotel on June 6, 1882, for George Webster Hearn, a native of Baltimore, Maryland. The service was conducted by Rev. Josiah Sims. Hearn had been ill for about a week before his untimely death. A longtime Nevada County resident, Hearn worked as a bartender in the National Hotel Saloon. On the same day Herman Naffziger's body lay in state at the Union Hotel after its arrival on the morning train from San Francisco. Sixty uniformed Knights of the Milo Lodge marched from their Castle Hall and conveyed the body to the Episcopal Church for the service. Both Naffziger and Hearn were laid to rest in Pine Grove Cemetery.

- In January of 1885 the old horse that had so long drawn the National Hotel bus was retired from service and a stronger, spryer and handsomer animal took its place.

- One of most bizarre stories connected with the National Hotel happened in November of 1882 when a lady from the county (her name was withheld) took a room at the hotel. At midnight W. A. Skidmore of San Francisco was on his way to his room on the same floor when he was accosted by the lady, who stuck her head out of her doorway and mistook him for a hotel employee. She asked Skidmore for another room because "There is too much gas in this one and it makes me feel kind of sick." She wanted a room without so much gas in it. The lady said that after retiring—and believing her asthma was getting worse than usual —she had decided that gas had caused the problem, and after throwing open the doors and windows and dressing in several layers of clothes, she sat up and waited for the room to air out. But it didn't. Mr. Skidmore asked if she had shut off the gas burner. She answered in the affirmative, saying, "Of course—I blew it out." Mr. Skidmore, a mining man, entered the room and quickly discovered the problem. After groping around in the dark Skidmore struck a match and applied it to the chandelier, causing a puff of light as big as a man's hat to appear. He explained to the lady that the proper method was to turn off the gas, not to blow it out like a candle. The story had a happy ending, with the lady narrowly escaping what might have proven disastrous to her—and the hotel as well.

12. The Golden Age of the Rector Brothers

In July of 1882 Elijah John (who went by John) and his brother, Bayliss S. Rector, followed longtime landlord Jacob Naffziger as the new proprietors at the Union Hotel on Main Street. The Union was then a large and grand wooden hotel and the National's main rival in Nevada City. The Rector brothers succeeded in building the business of the Union Hotel during the time of the "blighting influence of the Sawyer Decision" that almost completely shut down hydraulic mining in California and caused another period of depression.

Four years into their five-year lease of the Union Hotel, the Rector brothers also took over the National, so for a time the two leases overlapped and they operated both hotels. Up to this time the Rector brothers had more hotel experience than any of the previous owners or managers at the National Exchange. You might say they were born into the hotel business, as their father, the Hon. Jesse H. Rector, was the owner of a hotel in Elk Lick Springs, Pike County, Missouri, where he had also served as judge and postmaster. Both Jesse and their mother, the former Cynthia Simpson Strother, were natives of Fauquier County Virginia, and the brothers accompanied their parents on their westward migration to Missouri.

Their mother's family had been early settlers of California and brought a wagon train to the state in 1850 during the Gold Rush. One of the elder Rector's five daughters, Elizabeth, married Joseph Merritt, who became a California cattle dealer, while another daughter, Lucinda Jane, married Jefferson G. James, who became the owner of large tracts of land in California, amounting to over seventy thousand acres, and became the president of Fresno Loan and Savings Bank.

After graduating from college, Bayliss joined his father as a partner in the family's hotel, farming and stock business in Missouri. In 1873 Bayliss left for California and settled in

58

Stockton. He first worked for a year at the ranch of his brother-in-law, Jefferson James. Then, when his brother John came to California after working with their father for a time, the brothers moved to Hollister, California, where they went into the hotel business, forming the partnership of Rector Brothers in 1877. They managed the McMahon House prior to their move to Nevada City in 1882.

On June 26, 1880 the *North San Juan Times* published ads for the long-time rivals the Union and National Hotels in adjoining columns. This was something that the Nevada City newspapers would never have done.

On July 1, 1886, the Rector brothers became the proprietors of the National Hotel by leasing the building from Stanley Eddy, and in 1891 they purchased the property and hotel building. A publication reported that when the Rector Brothers took over the lease of the hotel it was in "rather a dilapidated condition and its patronage small."[1] It may have been in need of refurbishing due to normal wear and tear, but it is difficult to believe it was in *dilapidated* condition. Nevertheless, it suffered in comparison to the grandeur and modernization that the Rector brothers brought to the hotel in the next several years,

At the time Bayliss and John became the proprietors of the National they were already well-known and highly respected businessmen in Nevada City with a great deal of hotel experience behind them. In addition to running a first-class house, they were deeply involved in community service, were members of the local Elks, Odd Fellows and Knights of Pythias, and were influential in politics as well. Bayliss had held positions of county clerk, recorder and assessor during the time he lived in Hollister.

Perhaps the main reason the Rector brothers made the move from the Union Hotel to the National was that Broad street had become the business center of the city and was more important commercially now than Main Street. The advantageous location would be more profitable and more convenient and accessible for local townspeople and travelers alike.

Other sources say that the move was made because their lease on the Union Hotel would soon expire; perhaps the owner did not want to renew the lease now that the Union had become so popular and prosperous under the Rectors' management.

The three-story fire-proof National had 100 rooms at the time. It housed the head office for all of the stage lines leaving the city, the express office, and the post office. Also, several stores were under the roof of the National building, including a book store that conveniently sold stationery and supplies to travelers and guests. It certainly had many more amenities than most of the other smaller hotels in Nevada City or nearby towns.

1887 was a busy year for the Rector brothers. There were twice as many health and pleasure seekers visiting Nevada City that season than in any past year. Visitors came for the climate, water, scenery and the reputation of the good hotel accommodations in the town. A hotel as busy as the National suffered a great deal of daily wear and tear. Once the Rector brothers took over the management of the National they immediately began to repair, refurnish and repaint the hotel to the point where they could claim it was the best hotel north of Sacramento. There were many hotels between Sacramento and Nevada City, but large hotels with 100 rooms or more were few and far between.

One event that year which caused a particular excitement for the whole town was the night of August 3. The townspeople and visitors alike gathered in the streets in Nevada City "as men shouted themselves hoarse and the ladies waved handkerchiefs." The excitement was caused by two electric lights that were put into operation for the first time in town. One was suspended at Broad and Pine streets and the other near the bridge at the foot of Broad Street. Lights were also placed inside the National Hotel and several other businesses.[2]

Although electric lights were a welcome invention, in the beginning they were not reliable. The first power to the city was generated at the Rome power house, one the first hydroelectric projects in California. Edward Poorman, who had grown up in

Electric light above the intersection of Broad and Pine streets.

the area was a son of Samuel Poorman, a partner in the Middle Yuba Mining Company. Edward had visited Nevada City in his later years and stayed at the National Hotel, and had at one time lived at the Union Hotel. He recalled "The light bulbs were large clumsy affairs with big red filaments and would constantly come on and off. It was years before people started discarding their oil lamps."[3]

Some of the enhancements and upgrades at the National in 1887 included the addition of a large fire-proof safe installed in the office, a new large cooking stove in the kitchen, and Broad Street was paved with mine rock from the National to the Plaza bridge. This road improvement was paid for by individual business owners and was not the responsibility of the city. Thus street improvements were made in a patchwork approach, an ongoing problem for individual businessmen, and a nuisance for those who had to use streets full of potholes.

The pioneer Davies family arrived in Nevada County in the early years and Frank, along with his brothers Tom and Will, took over the operation of the livery stable and stage business between Forest City, Mountain House and Goodyear's Bar after

The Rector brothers: Elijah John and Bayliss Strother.

their father's death in 1890. After the Foote's Crossing Road was built, Frank operated the freight and mail stage between Forest City and Nevada City until 1935, and he owned one of the first automobiles in the county. From his headquarters in the National Hotel Frank chartered trips throughout the mountain area for mining men. He was also the man hired to dismantle and remove tracks, car barns and other equipment when the Nevada City and Grass Valley traction line was discontinued.

Frank Davies served two terms on the city council of Nevada City and was involved in many of the activities, including service for several years as chairman of the Fourth of July parade. He was instrumental in acquiring the Lake Vera site and helping to build the dam for the lake before it became a recreational and camping area for the several Camp Fire Girls units.

In 1894, when the Sunset Company established telephone lines between Nevada City and Grass Valley, the first office for the company was in the back room of Walter D. Vinton's drug store. The first telephone was installed at J. J. Jackson's store on Commercial Street. The second phone, with the telephone number of "2," was placed in the National Hotel.

Historian H. P. Davis wrote that the National Hotel was the birthplace of Pacific Gas and Electric Company. The story has been handed down through the years that during a meeting at the National Hotel in 1894 Eugene De Sabla and John Martin, pioneers in hydroelectric development, persuaded Romulus Riggs Colgate to join a combine of small electric and gas companies that eventually expanded and became P. G. and E.[4]

The Rector brothers advertised the National as the only *first-class* hotel in Nevada City inasmuch as it had the required number of rooms—no fewer than 70—and was a fire-proof structure.[5] They also claimed their dining room offered a "table" not to be excelled by any hotel in the interior of the state.

In the meantime, the Nevada County Board of Trade (predecessor of the Nevada County Promotion Committee in which the Rector brothers were active members, and the later Chamber of Commerce) in the 1890s was touting Nevada County's natural features and unique advantages by placing this advertisement in various publications, including the local paper:[6]

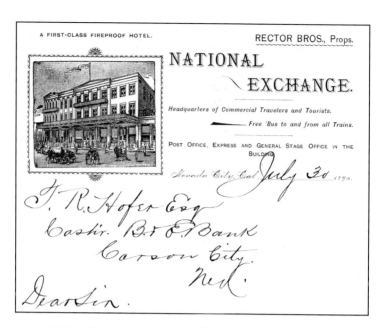

National Exchange stationery from the summer of 1895.

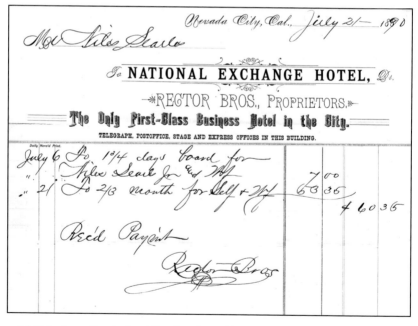

A bill for boarding Judge Niles Searls and his wife for part of a month, and their son and daughter-in-law for a couple of days, in 1890.

First: Large areas of fertile land, secured by Government Patent can be purchased at reasonable prices—a small farm can be purchased for a few hundred dollars

Second: The fruits grown in the county are the finest varieties grown in the world with a superior flavor and firm texture that give them better shipping and keeping qualities than those grown at lower altitudes. Grown in the county are: oranges, lemons, citrons, figs, olives, apricots, plums, strawberries, blackberries, raspberries, gooseberries, hazel nuts, black walnuts, chestnuts, almonds, and every kind of vegetable known.

Third: The long summers permit the rotation of crops and the raising of two and three crops from the same land in a single season.

Fourth: There is a ready market for all farm products at good prices.

Fifth: There is an excellent means of transportation to the railway via the Narrow Gauge Rail Road to the main lines connecting at Colfax.

Sixth: There is an abundance of timber.

Seventh: There is an inexhaustible supply of pure water for irrigating and domestic use.

Eighth: The temperature is mild both in summer and winter and not subject to sudden changes.

Ninth: The climate compares favorably with that of any other area on the Pacific Coast, there being no malaria, no violent winds, no fogs or floods.

Tenth: The children reared in this climate and altitude above the sea usually acquire better physical constitutions and better fitness and development than those reared in the valley or coastal counties.

In the mid 1890s there were five daily newspapers, one tri-weekly and three weeklies published in Nevada County, which had a population of 25,000. The county also boasted the richest gold mines for employment (including quartz, hydraulic and placer mines), even with restrictions on hydraulic mining by the much hated Sawyer Decision.

In 1896 Bayliss Rector was elected mayor of Nevada City. In that same year the Rector brothers applied to the city trustees for permission to build an elevated brick passageway from the

65

second story of the National Hotel to the second floor of a new brick building on the other side of a narrow alley. To make room for the new structure, some old wooden buildings would be torn down and Rectors told the trustees the new building would add greatly to the appearance of lower Broad street.

After the trustees granted their application the Rector brothers immediately hired local architect Ira Fancher. On August 18, 1896, a notice in the *Daily Transcript* invited contractors to submit sealed bids to construct a three-story brick building at the corner of Broad Street and National Alley. Apparently the original plan proved too costly, and a two-story wooden structure was erected by the firm of Crider, Wilson and McKenzie. The new building had a footprint of 50 x 120 feet. The second story, which was connected with the main hotel by an enclosed bridged walkway, contained sixteen new sleeping rooms, including some suites and bathrooms. Each bedroom featured stationary wash stands with hot and cold running water.

The ground floor of the new annex contained a sales room 48 x 60 feet with a full plate-glass front. In the rear were two 24 x 40 foot sample rooms for the convenience of commercial travelers. It was customary in those days for salesmen (known as "drummers") to travel from town to town, and either take orders for their firms from local merchants or place advertisements in the newspapers and sell direct to the public. All the rooms of the new annex were electrified.

The grand opening and reception for the new annex began at 7:30 p.m. at the National on the evening of July 23, 1897. The event opened with an open-air concert by Goyne's Band on the balcony of the main hotel, and then the band played for dancing from 10:00 until after 1:00 o'clock. A short address was given by Judge Julius M. Walling, after which the large crowd was entertained with songs, recitations and selections on the piano while refreshments were served to all the guests.

Photo of Broad Street and the National Hotel taken sometime after
the electric trolley line was installed in 1901.

Old post card showing the stage arrival at the National Hotel. In the middle
of Broad Street is a Nevada County Traction Company trolley.

13. The New Era: 1900

1900 WAS A BUSY YEAR in Nevada City as the town was bustling with visitors keeping merchants and businesses active. Especially busy were contractors, architects and anyone in the building trades. Three large projects would be responsible for wagon-loads of building material moving in and around the town and business district.

Two of the projects were planned—and another was an unexpected near-disaster. In early February Mayor Bayliss Rector suggested to the city trustees that a plan be adopted to fix and improve the streets of the city. He brought to their attention that the current method of having each property owner repair his own piece of street was slow and impracticable. In order to secure satisfactory results, the city should assume responsibility for all street work, to be paid for from a fund created for that purpose. He suggested the issuance of bonds in order to raise the funds necessary to put the streets in first-class shape in a timely manner.

In the same month the county supervisors met in a special session where they had received the plans and specifications to remodel and add a third-story to the Nevada County court house to make it a larger and more up-to-date building. First, and most important, the entire building was to be fireproofed. A new boiler room was to be added to heat the entire building from an excavation at the rear of the assessor's office. The wooden front of the portico, including the wooden columns, would be removed and replaced with an iron railing on the front of the porch. The third-story would have five windows, iron cornices and a fireproof sheet-steel roof. The first and second story interiors would be completely remodeled, and a new third floor would hold the courtroom, judge's chambers, jury room and offices for the district attorney, sheriff and superintendent of schools.[1]

To fit the special needs of hilly Nevada City, the first of several fire towers designed by firemen was placed in service by May 1909. These towers had been built and installed from the firehouse fund, without cost to the city. There were six steel towers from 30 to 60 feet in height, varying because of the location where they were installed. Each tower was equipped with a 2 ½" water pipe that led to the top of the tower where it was connected with a revolving *monitor* capable of throwing a stream of water in whatever direction it was aimed—up, down or in a complete circle. It was claimed that if all of the towers were in operation at the same time their range would overlap and distribute a blanket of water over the heart of Nevada City. One fire chief said, "A man on top of a tower was worth six men on the ground during a blaze." [2]

The towers thus had acquired the nickname of "Guardian Angels." One tower was located in the rear of the National Hotel; one on top of the Alpha Hardware store on Broad Street; another on a platform on Main Street above the Forest Service warehouses; one in the back of the Miners Foundry on Spring Street; a fifth on the Masonic Building on Pine Street and the sixth near the Chinese laundry on Commercial Street.

Nevada City view around the turn of the century shows the old Union Hotel on Main Street (the white building just right of center below Sugar Loaf) prior to the fire that burned the hotel on February 13, 1900.

On February 13th the dreaded cry and alarm of fire was heard at the three-story wood-frame Union Hotel on Main Street. If not for the quick work of several fire companies, a good, steady water flow, hard-working firemen and a large number of citizens who pitched in, nearby buildings might easily have caught fire and spread to the rest of the business district. The roof and the entire third floor of the Union Hotel were a complete loss, and water damage, ash and smoke caused additional destruction to the lower floors.

Later, a faulty flume was guessed to be the cause of the fire, although the evidence was not conclusive. The next day's newspapers called the Union Hotel a mass of ruins, but directors of the Citizens Bank, which held notes on the property, met the next week to determine if the hotel should be rebuilt. At the time of the fire the Union was under the management of Henry Metzenbaugher and it was agreed by the bank that under his control the hotel was running profitably. In fact, it was said that the business was the best it had been for a number of years. A contract was awarded immediately to local contractor, George Hughes, to remodel and modernize the hotel, adding many improvements throughout the building in the process.

In March of 1900 the *The Daily Transcript* mentioned that *Harper's Weekly* contained an article on the National Hotel which might have been responsible for a good many of the tourists who visited Nevada City that season. The article described the bar in particular:

> One of the curious sights in California which every traveler goes to see is the bar in the principal hotel at Nevada City, made out of California laurel. This bar was placed there in 1864. The hotel has been rebuilt several times since, but the bar has been taken out and always put back in the new hotel.
>
> L. D. Calkins [part owner of the *Transcript*], who went to California before the '49er's says that over $8,000,000 has passed over the counter of this bar—the largest sum of money that has passed over any bar in the same period of thirty-five years. The wooden top of the bar was something like eight inches thick when it was first built. Now it is worn down to less than two inches.[3]

In the same month the Rector brothers were fined $30 by Judge Coughlin for keeping their barroom open till after 12:00 o'clock.

The biggest event at the National Hotel that year came in June when, after a great deal of hammering, and sawing, the tradesmen had completed their work. Although improvements and innovations at the National were standard, there was an extra special zeal and energy as workers were seen everywhere in the hotel up to and throughout June. New carpets, furniture, wallpaper and general conveniences were spruced-up or replaced.

In the parlors of the National Hotel on June 27 Libby Rector, the only daughter of Bayliss and Susan Griffin Rector, was married to city attorney Irenaeus Cory Lindley. The hotel was decorated inside and out with evergreens, smilax and Chinese lanterns, while the parlors were decorated with sweet peas, carnations and asparagus fern, with decorations of pink. After the marriage a bridal supper was held for family and immediate relatives, and a large reception held later that evening at 9:00 p.m. with cake and ice cream served and dancing on the hotel balcony. After the big event was over and summer came to a close the popularity of the hotel did not decline, nor did the business that continued throughout the fall season.

That summer the hotel was exceedingly busy with tourists, mining men, commercial travelers and all other classes of the traveling public, as the hotel's reputation spread up and down California. Even with the new annex all the rooms were continually filled and the hotel had to resort to the use of "outside rooms" every night.

While business was brisk at the National there was a new business that appeared to be equally popular, one that was causing a lot of attention in the neighborhood. City trustees and merchants were not happy about it, nor were the Rector brothers, whose hotel was in close proximity.

At the December 3rd board of trustees meeting Mayor Rector made a "strong" statement regarding the house of ill-fame that had recently opened on Spring Street—thirty-feet from that part of the National Hotel where he and his family and many ladies and children were sleeping. The mayor went on to explain that the noises and disturbances made by people going to and from these houses were a continual annoyance.[4] Evidence was given by night watchman James Neagle about the bad language and disturbances that had recently occurred in back of the National.

The current situation in the city, was that houses of ill-fame were being operated on Spring Street and upper Commercial Street in violation of the old city ordnance that prohibited such businesses on Broad, Pine or Commercial streets. Mayor Rector requested that his proposed ordinance be read. It would ban houses of prostitution from either side of Spring Street or National Alley. The original ordinance failed to pass because not all of the trustees were present and Clerk Peard was unwilling to cast the deciding vote. The ordinance then was amended to disallow houses of prostitution on the *north* side of Spring Street and on both sides of National Alley. This met with Peard's approval and the amended ordinance was adopted.

Two days later Mrs. Coughlin spoke to *The Union* and denied that she was conducting her house on National Alley as a bawdy house, as had been alleged at the trustees' meeting.[5]

The newly rebuilt and remodeled Union Hotel opened the first week of January 1901, and manager Henry Metzenbaugher announced that the 100 sunny rooms were newly furnished and the hotel had been repaired and repainted throughout. He insisted that his hotel had the largest modern dining room, making it second to no hotel in that part of the state.

During the same week National Hotel offered free lunches at its bar immediately following the Elk's Minstrels performances —everyone was invited to attend the festivities. One of the new updates at the National that season was its large steam table: "a modern device for keeping food and dishes hot during their service—a truly up-to-date improvement."[6]

In March John Rector's wife Margaret (sister to the wife of his brother Bayliss) died after suffering from a lingering illness.

Nevada County Bank Incorporated

In December of the previous year the Nevada County Bank had been formed and incorporated at Grass Valley by a group of San Francisco capitalists, in combination with the Rector brothers, their sons, Gilbert James and Elijah Merritt Rector, William

H. Martin of the Miners Foundry, and George W. Starr of the Empire mine. In April 1901 John Rector purchased considerable stock and was chosen president; his son Gilbert became the head cashier.

A few months later the Rector brothers again announced plans for major improvements to the National. Part of the reason may have been that John Rector was trying to keep busy after the death of his wife. The plans called for an entire renovation of the original hotel and the installation of the latest modern conveniences. It included addition of another story in the rear of the hotel over the kitchen, to be divided into rooms for the accommodation of the employees. Additional skylights were to be installed for greater light in all the rooms, smaller rooms enlarged, porcelain baths installed in all the suites, and hot and cold water and steam radiators for the entire building. The dining room would be enlarged and several small buildings added to the back of the hotel. New carpets and the latest furnishings were being placed in most of the rooms.

A few months later a large plate-glass front was installed at the east end of the National where Miss Anne Cohen's variety store, and Wells, Fargo and Co.'s office was located. The contract for the first phase of the extensive remodeling and refurbishment was awarded to Walter Lewis. It would take the next two years for all of the work to be completed.

The Rector brothers seemed to find frequent occasions to throw a party and invite not only everyone in the city but also extend their invitation to everyone in the county. It is no wonder their reputation was well-known to mining and commercial people as well as to the traveling public.

In June of 1903 the Rector brothers celebrated the seventeenth anniversary of their management of the National Hotel and annex with an open-air concert and dance on the 130-foot-long porch that was decorated lavishly with greens and ferns around all sides and colored electric lights hung from every branch. Long before the announced time of festivities the hotel began to get crowded and the place was filled almost to capacity. Hundreds were unable to gain admittance because the sidewalk was blocked by the crowd that had gathered in the front of the hotel doorway. Punch and lemonade were served, and at 11 o'clock several summer-time favorites were offered, including sherbets and ice cream.

In August of 1904 another anniversary celebration was held in honor of the Rector brothers' twenty-second anniversary in the hotel business at Nevada City (including their time at the Union Hotel). Once again the hotel was opened to the public, and all were invited to the reception and dance. For this event the balcony was decorated with incandescent lights and Japanese lanterns, and light refreshments were served in the dining room, which was decorated with evergreens and flowers. The parlors were given over to the ladies in attendance and the card rooms and tables offered whist, euchre and other card games.

Perhaps my favorite National hotel nugget is the "Spoon Came Back" story that was published in *The Union* on December 16, 1906.

> All over the country hotels and restaurants suffer the loss of silverware, particularly of spoons, knives and forks, which bear the monogram of the place. People take them for souvenirs and the loss in time amounts to thousands of dollars. The National has been no exception, but one lady who took a couple of spoons last summer became conscience stricken and returned the spoons, sending the following letter with them:
>
> "I am sending you under separate cover two teaspoons, which belong to your hotel, [that I took] for souvenirs, but I have come to the conclusion since then that it was not the proper thing to do, so I am returning them."

A few months before the Rector brothers celebrated thirty years in business in Nevada County and twenty-five at the National Hotel, an event was held there that was probably a first in the lives of both the hotel and the hotel owners.

Unidentified couple on the National Hotel balcony overlooking Broad Street.

The Fourth of July parade in 1910 featured many horse and rider entries.

14. Superior Court Held in the National Hotel

EVENTS AND MEETINGS of Nevada City's social and fraternal life were held at the National over the years just as they continue to this day. A Superior Court trial was moved to the National for the first—and probably only—time in April of 1912.

A problem was encountered in the sensational and high-profile Nevada City murder trial of Paul M. Doyle on Monday, April 1st—and it was no April Fool's joke. Cora Rule, a trained nurse who had cared for William H. M. Smith (the alleged victim) from the time he was wounded until his death, had come from Truckee to give testimony. Mrs. Rule, who was staying at the National Hotel, had been present when Smith gave a dying statement about the circumstances of his shooting. During her testimony from a wheel chair, it was stipulated that Mrs. Rule was ill and might need an operation.

Court was adjourned for lunch, but when the afternoon session opened she was unable to continue due to severity of her illness. The next morning Mrs. Rule was unable to go to the court house and too ill to sit up. The court moved to the parlor of the National Hotel, where court officials, jury, attorneys and spectators crowded around a couch where Mrs. Rule was reclining. After her testimony ended the judge, jury, attorneys and spectators moved back to the courthouse to resume the trial.[1]

William Smith, who managed and edited the *Truckee Republican* and owned the Whitney House at Truckee, was put into the nurse's care after he being shot twice with a Colt 32 revolver by Doyle, a merchant who owned the Truckee electric-power plant. The incident took place at the Truckee post office, where the two had gone to pick up their mail. Doyle fired five or six shots at Smith, two of which hit Smith, leaving him paralyzed. Assistant district attorney Francis M. Rutherford (whose wife was postmistress) was in the inner room of the post office when he heard loud voices and several pistol shots.

There had been an on-going feud of a long duration between the two men because Smith had used his newspaper to crusade against the Truckee saloons and gambling. A rival paper, *The Truckee Independent,* was launched in opposition to the *Republican,* and Smith was said to have received proof that Doyle was its principal backer.

Doyle, a wealthy merchant, leading citizen and member of a prominent Truckee family, had formerly operated the town's bank. He was owner of a large store in Truckee, the power plant, and a new resort at Donner Lake. Although Doyle did not operate a saloon, he was known to be a silent partner with Jim May, the former part-owner of the Palace gambling house in Reno. Doyle was also a prominent Mason, being a Knight Templar of the lodge in Truckee.

From the time of the shooting the case had many twists and turns. Justice of the Peace Lee Adolph of Truckee Township refused to conduct the preliminary hearing, stating the Doyle was a close friend of his and a member of the same fraternity. District Attorney Arbogast said he would ask for the resignation of Adolph as justice of the peace if he refused to comply

with the request, and he would ask the Nevada County Board of Supervisors to remove Adolph for neglect of duty. Doyle retained attorney Charles F. McGlashan of Truckee to represent him through the preliminary trial. After the death of Smith, Arbogast charged Doyle with first-degree murder and he would be the chief prosecutor in the case of the People of the State of California versus Paul M. Doyle.

It was almost impossible to seat a jury. Due to the pre-trial publicity there were few men in the county who had not already made up their minds about Doyle's guilt or innocence or were willing to consider a death verdict. The trial had more than fifty witnesses testify, witnesses for each side offering contradicting evidence and testimony about the two men.

After three votes and only four hours of deliberation the jury found Doyle not guilty. The jury apparently believed that Smith instigated the altercation at the post office and Doyle was defending himself from Smith. However, there was no additional gun or other threatening implement found at the scene except Doyle's weapon.

An event to honor the Rector brothers and celebrate their thirty years in the hotel business was the last big celebration the brothers would share. Maybe not so strangely, the Rector brothers passed away within a year of each other.

On July 7, 1914, Elijah John Rector died in his apartment at the National Hotel after a three-day illness caused by complications of heart disease and "acute muscular rheumatism." His sudden death shocked his family and friends.

Less than a year later, on May 1, 1915, Bayliss also died in his apartments at the National Hotel, after an illness of several months caused by heart and kidney trouble.[2] With the death of these men the golden age may have passed into history, but the firm would now be in the hands of the next generation of Rector brothers—Gilbert and Merritt, sons of John Rector—along with Bayliss's widow, Susan Rector, and daughter, Vivie Rector Lindley.

Gilbert James Rector, oldest son of John and Margaret Rector.

Edwin Merritt Rector, second son of John and Margaret Rector.

A Succession of Managers at the National

Two months after John Rector's death the firm of Rector Brothers announced they had leased the National to William D. Watson, former manager of the Hotel Maywood in Corning, Tehama County, California, who came highly recommended. The younger Rector brothers had decided it would be impossible for them to devote personal attention to both the hotel and the Nevada County Bank without the help of either John or Bayliss Rector. The lease given to Watson involved only the hotel business and not the various stores that were located in the National Hotel.

Watson wrote to his wife after he had settled in at the hotel in October 1915. She was living still in Redding, waiting for their successors to take over at Corning before she could join him, and he complained to her that due to poor management he saw a great deal of problems—especially in the kitchen, where he thought the Rectors had been wasting hundreds of dollars worth of food each month. According to Watson, the office help was "rotten," and he thought the whole house (except for of the dining room girls and chambermaids and one bar man) would have

Trolley tracks down the center of busy Broad Street. The National Hotel appears on the left and Alpha Hardware is on the right.

to be replaced. He did not find the rooms to be as good as expected—but supposed they could still rent out the "poor" rooms for fifty cents a night.

In November Watson moved his family to Nevada City and for a short time he went into business with W. E. Tuttle of that city, whom he may have known prior to relocating. Later Watson bought out Tuttle's interest.

One important change Watson made after he became the manager of the National was to abandon the American Hotel Plan, where patrons were charged a fixed fee that included room and meals (whether you ate them or not) in favor of the European Plan, where guests paid separately for meals. This may have been his way to eliminate the large food waste that he claimed was occurring in the kitchen.

In July 1916 Watson announced that a new grill service was available in the large bar room. A merchant lunch, served all day from 9 a.m. to midnight, became very popular. It included soup, salad, a choice of meats, vegetables, dessert, and a choice between coffee, tea, wine or beer—all for thirty-five cents.

In addition to other changes Watson made in the hotel, he took over the Central House (across from the National) for additional rooms. Watson was an experienced businessman and became active in the social and commercial life and was a strong supporter of the Nevada City Chamber of Commerce.

William Watson had been the manager of the National little over a year when he had a small accident that injured one of his fingers in a doorway at the hotel in December of 1916. Shortly thereafter he suffered an ulcerated tooth which resulted in an acute infection that caused a lump to form in his neck. He was taken to the Jones Memorial Hospital, where his condition seemed to improve until he developed pneumonia and had complications from a weak heart; after failing to respond to treatment he died unexpectedly on December 7 at the age of 45.

Watson was a member of the Redding, California Lodge, No. 1073, BPOE, and a service for him was held at the Nevada City Elks Lodge where Gilbert Rector delivered the eulogy and his body lay in state. Since the Watson family had lived in Nevada County for such a short time he was not buried here. His body was shipped to San Francisco, where his parents and one sister lived, and his body was cremated and interred at Cypress Lawn Cemetery.

After William Watson's death, his widow, Alma Jones Watson, and their three daughters were unable to manage the hotel alone. The Rector brothers announced on December 31 that they would again take over the hotel, which would revert to the American Plan as in years before.

Two Close Calls by Fire

Rector Bros. next hired Joseph H. O'Connor to manage the hotel. The native son of Nevada County, born at Lake City and formerly of North Bloomfield, where he had been in the mercantile business with A. R. Morrison, O'Connor had a diverse combination of business and management skills. He had been the superintendent of the Union Blue mine above North Bloomfield for a time. Then he was employed by the Hammond engineering company and spent several years working in Arizona, Colorado and New Mexico. O'Connor had recently managed a hotel in San Francisco (also named the National) that was a popular gathering place for Nevada County visitors while in that city. O'Connor came to Nevada City in January 1917 to take over management of the National Exchange Hotel.

While Joseph O'Connor was manager there were two fires that could have proved disastrous for the hotel. A close call came on evening of July 11, 1918, when a fire was discovered in the roof of the rear wing of the hotel about 9:30 p.m. and the entire roof of that wing was ablaze by the time the alarm was sent out. It had apparently burned for some time in the attic storeroom before it was discovered, and the cause of the fire was undetermined. The fire company said it was one of the hardest fires the local department had contended with for some time.

Firemen used two hoses to attack the fire from the outside with streams of water aimed on the roof, and took a third hose up the narrow stairway to the attic. The fight in the storeroom was very dangerous with heavy smoke and bad air. It took an hour to combat the flames. A woman guest from San Francisco told *The Morning Union* that although she had seen many fires in San Francisco and elsewhere, she never had witnessed men plunging right into the fire as the Nevada City men did, and they were credited with saving the hotel.

Considerable damage resulted from the fire, largely from water. In addition to the roof, the kitchen, laundry, storeroom and fourteen guest rooms were soaked with water.

A little less than a year later, on June 18, 1919, a fire was discovered at 7:00 p.m., believed to have been smoldering for a long time before the flames broke through the iron roof and large amounts of smoke were seen pouring into the night sky. Fire companies and engines rushed to the scene, where they soon had several lines of water spraying the fire, and as quickly as possible got the fire under control. The fire was prevented from spreading to other parts of the building, but it took an hour to chop through the building and rip off the iron roofing in order to extinguish the flames.

By this time the kitchen, dining room and the upper floor facing Pine Street had been completely drenched with water. The fire may have started from the flue, although that was only a guess. The firemen again saved the day, but there were two injuries suffered by them: James Penrose's finger was cut to the bone and A. M. Holmes' face was badly scorched.

Either because of the recent two fires or by mutual agreement between Rector Brothers and O'Connor, Abraham L. Leam and Thomas C. Hopkins were the new managers at the National Hotel by year's end. Leam, born in Pennsylvania, was 54 years old; Hopkins, 44 years old, was born in Ohio. Not much else is known about either of them, and they managed the hotel for only two or three years.

In 1921 O'Connor was appointed superintendent of the county hospital by the board of supervisors. He worked there with his wife Mary, who was the matron until his death in February 1924.

By January of 1923 Edward E. Leichter took control of the hotel.[3] Born in the state of Nevada, he accompanied his parents to California in 1850, where his father mined for several years before moving to Virginia City, Nevada, to work as a metallurgist and chemist until his death. Edward Leichter went to local schools in Nevada and completed his education in San Francisco, afterward working four year for the Union Iron Works as a mechanical engineer. He was employed by several mining companies in both California and Nevada. After an enlistment in the Army when he spent some time in the Philippines, he returned to the United States to again work in the mining industry. In 1915 he took over the Alpha Garage on Main Street, Nevada City, where automobiles were repaired, stored and rented. With his background in mechanical and mining affairs he must have been popular with guests who had mining interests and business to conduct in Nevada City.

By January of 1925 Lola M. Kolker and Vivie Rector Lindley were being advertised as the managers of the hotel, but by October of that year Lola M. Kolker was the lone manager. Then, on November first the Rector brothers and Mrs. Lindley announced that Fred C. Worth, a well-known grocery commercial traveler, had leased the National for five years and would be assisted by Mrs. Lola Kolker.

Looking down Broad Street in the early 1930s.

15. Fred Worth and a Modernized Hotel

WORTH'S PLAN SEEMED to be more in line with that of the Rector brothers of old: to run a first-class modern hotel, catering to families, tourists, mining men, commercial travelers and the general public. The Rectors probably were hopeful that under Worth's management the National would resume its earlier reputation and develop increased business. A mining revival was currently underway in the region, and Fred Worth had plans for various improvements to the hotel as business conditions warranted.

Some major changes took place, beginning in January 1926. The historic old barroom that had been in service for over half a century was remodeled to became the new modern coffee shop. The large space was divided and in the rear area a space 18 by 40 feet became the new kitchen. A wall was put up to divide the dining room area from the kitchen to keep cooking odors from "discomforting the patrons," and the storerooms that formerly were in the back of bar room were used for refrigeration.

After renovations were started it was learned that, in order to complete the coffee shop, the forty-year-old barber shop had to be moved because of where the building supports were located. The barber shop was a place that had seen generations of family men, and hundreds of miners and visitors, shaved, trimmed and groomed, William Reynolds, the current barber, had worked in the present location since 1911. He had taken over the shop from the former barber, William Walter, a master barber whose reputation was known for miles around, and was an early Nevada City pioneer.

The shop's dark old oak chairs, ornate chandeliers and the waiting area furniture (worn and molded into comfortable shapes through time) were removed to make room for the new and modern. This aged barber shop had seen "the wonder of the hair bobbing fad of the female sex sweep through the country as well as the stiff crops of whiskers come and be shorn, and had seen the locks of the hardy mountaineers fall before the snip of the shears." [1]

Although barber Reynolds had to relinquish the old familiar location that was known from one end of the state to the other, he soon found a new location nearby. The old barber chairs and other furnishings and equipment were moved to the Schreiber Block at Broad and Pine streets. (The Schreiber Block had replaced the U.S. Hotel after the 1856 fire.) The new shop was painted a bright white, and the furniture and all the fixtures were enameled to match. A large plate-glass window looking out to Broad street provided the new shop with plenty of light and added to its new modern look. The relocated barber shop opened a month before the new National Hotel coffee shop. The first customer was Judge Julius M. Walling, who for nearly fifty years had been a customer at the former location.

Meanwhile, the view after walking in the front door of the coffee shop was of the new soda fountain and lunch counters, configured in a U shape in the center of the room. The historic National bar was remodeled and used as one of the counters. Several small tables were arranged around the room, as well as several booths installed for those who desired more privacy. Mirrors hung on the walls, while the front exterior was remodeled so that it conformed with the hotel front. Large windows with specially designed lighting faced Broad Street. The coffee shop could be entered from the hotel lobby through French doors newly installed for the convenience of hotel guests. New hours of operation were from 6:00 a.m. until 11:00 p.m.,

Any major changes to the National would normally warrant an eventful premiere. Although the completed coffee shop was opened to the public first on March 25, a formal grand opening was delayed until April 10 so the serving staff could familiarize themselves with the new shop, which had a seating capacity of about 75 to 80 customers

A section of the old dining room upstairs was retained for large gatherings. With fifty lights and a large mirror that ran nearly half the length of the room, it was bright and pleasant, a big change from the era of the dark Victorian dining room.

The *Union* newspaper reported:

A pleasant glass front adjacent to the hotel entrance gives the new shop a smart touch with an air of refinement and cleanliness when the spick and span interior is viewed. A pleasant effect of softness and harmony has been achieved through polychrome decorating, this scheme being carried throughout. On one side are set chummy booths, each with individual lights. Individual tables are properly spaced in the floor center while the right side is flanked with the proper lunch counter. A spotless kitchen is one of the features of the new shop, but due to hiding partitions this is not displayed to the public but may be inspected at any time."[2]

The formal opening of the coffee shop on April 10th, like most of the past public events held at the National, was notable and grand. The Worths hired a four-piece orchestra for the affair, and floral arrangements to decorate the hotel lobby and coffee shop were provided by the Worths' many local and out-of-town friends. To add to the festive atmosphere, many local people came to the opening wearing formal wear and masks from the Chamber of Commerce's Masquerade Ball, held the same evening.

Twenty-five rooms had been repapered, repainted and refurnished, and new suites and rooms with baths were completed, with future plans to include a bath in every room. The old lobby was transformed to provide a bright and modern entrance to the hotel. New wallpaper was hung, woodwork repainted and a cozy corner created to the right of the entrance for letter writing. Across the room desk-tables were placed opposite the new counter, and carpets and sofas were arranged around the room for the comfort of guests. The old space used by the telegraph company was moved to the back of the room, and the stage office and the "cluttering that was a part of it" were removed.

The final improvement was the installation of telephones in many of the rooms. The hotel switchboard had the capacity to connect 100 telephones, and eventually almost all rooms at the National were connected the office and the outside world.

Fred Worth was applauded for the large investment and improvements he had made—it was said that those who enjoyed the

National's hospitality in the "good old days" would fail to recognize the hotel as the same place. It was a boost to the city, and gave the hotel a reputation for being progressive and up-to-date.

It may not have been a surprise to local businessmen and the community when it was announced in September of 1927 that after forty-one years the company known as Rector Brothers had sold the National Hotel building and its contents to the Worths, who been leasing it for two years. During the Rector era the hotel had been the center of social and other activities in Nevada City, and many business ideas were first conceived in informal meetings or small gatherings at the National Hotel.

Fires Visit Broad Street

On July 21, 1928, a fire broke out in the early morning hours in the interior of the Alpha building across from the National Hotel on Broad street. Flames from the fire shot up over 100 feet in the air and the Nevada City fire department was soon joined by Grass Valley fire companies to combat the fire. As the blaze spread to the roofs of the Odd Fellows building, Hogan's shoe store, Schreiber's building at Pine and Broad streets, the building of William Harry on the corner of Pine and Spring streets, the buildings of Tommy Jennings and the Nevada City Cleaners, next to the Alpha building, all were on fire for a time. Luckily, there no wind was blowing or it would have spread far and wide.

Miss Springer, the night operator of the Pacific Telephone and Telegraph Co. became suspicious when lights on her switchboard for the Alpha building lit up, indicating that the circuit for the telephones at the Alpha was open. Soon the lights were flashing and, realizing that this must have been caused by a fire, she immediately rang city hall and then the National Hotel to tell night clerk A. D. Keller that she believed there was a fire in the Alpha store.

Mr. Keller looked across the street and was able to see the flames inside the front window of the store. He called his boss, Fred Worth, and Fred Cassidy of Alpha Hardware. After notifying W. L. Mobley, another hotel clerk of the emergency, Keller quickly went through the hotel alerting the guests of the fire across the street and asking them to prepare for possible evacu-

A fire occured on July 21, 1928, in the Alpha Hardware Stores building directly opposite the National Hotel in the downtown business district.

ation. The Alpha building, built of reinforced concrete, had been considered to be fire safe and the finest commercial building in the city, but it was destroyed except for the four outer walls left standing after the fire was extinguished.

It was a close call for the newly remodeled National. The front of the hotel was badly scorched, so that the entire front of the hotel had to be repainted. This work was completed several months later in early November. Little did anyone guess that before the month was out another morning fire would erupt on Broad Street, and this time the National would not be so fortunate.

Another Fire—the Pride of Nevada City Burns

On the morning of November 26, 1928, the townspeople awoke to the acrid smell of smoke in the air and discovered the mass of blackened ruins of what had been the "pride of the city, —the modern National Hotel Coffee Shop, only a little over three years old. The fire broke out in the early morning hours; smoke began pouring into the coffee shop, and gas from the refrigerator caused a loud explosion. Charles Ninnis, the night clerk, hearing the explosion, located the fire and called the operator of the night exchange to report it.

By the time firemen arrived the kitchen was fully engulfed,

so firemen sounded one alarm at the firebox in front of Harris's Pharmacy and sounded a second alarm a few minutes later. Fire hoses were brought in from the hydrant in front of the post office: one through the front door of the coffee shop, one through the hotel lobby, another through the side door of the coffee shop. An additional line was carried up and over Dickerman's drug store on an extension ladder to the roof of the hotel to fight the blaze in the wooden extension behind the hotel. Other lines were run from the back of the hotel at the corner of Spring street and National Alley through the courtyard of the hotel. Two additional lines from Pine and Spring street were brought into the kitchen from a side entrance and through a third-story window in the rear of the wooden extension.

When flames in the kitchen and coffee shop areas had been extinguished, it was discovered that the fire had taken a strange turn. The ground floor fire had been so hot that it burst through the west wall, traveled up the wooden wall for two stories into the attic of the wooden building and was well underway before it was discovered. Thus the firemen had a second fire to extinguish, with the possibility of the fire spreading throughout the hotel along the hotel's maze of hallways. The fire was suppressed by the iron roof at that point, but the smoke had no way to escape, and the flames were pushed along the length of the wood building, making the fire very difficult for firefighters to combat.

The firemen labored diligently and, by working from the roof of the brick building they were able to pry some of the iron roof off the wood building to allow the smoke to escape and permit them to fight the flames. At first a major obstacle was the large volume of dangerous gas mixed with chemicals that made breathing difficult. Many complained of pains in their lungs from inhaling the gas.

Several positive factors assisted in combating the fires. First was the recently purchased 800 feet of fire hose. Another was a city code that prohibited parking of automobiles on the streets of the city after 2:00 a.m. That cleared the street of vehicles, allowing firemen to move and handle the fire lines without obstructions.

Early speculation attributed the fire to wires to the refrigerator short-circuiting in the kitchen at the rear of the coffee shop and igniting an area between the ceiling and the upstairs dining room of the hotel. The walls of the hotel in this area were brick and most of the kitchen built out of stone. Although the guest rooms suffered no fire damage, the delay before the iron roof was removed caused an immense amount of water to seep down through the rooms, loosening plaster and ruining décor and furnishings.

Damage to the coffee shop, kitchen, the old upstairs dining room and guest rooms was estimated to be over $20,000, much more than their insured amount. Most of the furnishings and equipment could be replaced and the rooms refurbished. The biggest loss was a long mirror with two statues on each side that had been placed in the coffee shop. These were believed to be original to the earliest bar room when the National first opened. A replacement mirror, it was said, could "never hold the same place in the affections of the people."[3]

The ruins were still smoking when plans for rebuilding were made. Mr. Worth told *The Union* newspaper that, although the damage was severe, he would undertake reconstruction as soon as possible, because he had confidence in Nevada City and the National as well as the future of the community. He thanked and credited the "boys" of the department for their efficient efforts which prevented a holocaust of worse proportions. Worth told the reporter no expense or pains would be spared to equip the National with an eating place that was the peer of any in this part of California.

A mere week later Worth had the upstairs dining room repaired and put in working condition. He brought tables and chairs upstairs and then concentrated on restoring the coffee shop downstairs. A crew began to tear out the plaster and remove damaged material. Time was valuable, for quickly approaching was one of the busiest times of the year, the Christmas and New Year holidays.

Renovations were completed as rapidly as possible, and by mid-December Worth announced that the coffee shop would reopen on New Year's Eve. That night would also be the twenty-second annual Firemen's Ball and Masquerade at the Red

Men's Hall and the firemen who worked so valiantly to save the National from complete destruction would celebrate with Worth in his grand reopening. Reservations were being taken for "not less than four persons at a table, and for as many more at a table as desired." Booths in the coffee shop held four, and the price per couple for that night was five dollars, which would include a hot plate supper.

That night the upstairs dining room held an orchestra for dancing between the serving of the courses of dinner, as well as a celebration of the reopening. The Worths received many well wishes and floral pieces from friends and hotel employees. The coffee-shop booths and tables were reserved for the evening to handle the overflow, and the new lunch counter was used to accommodate dancers from the firemen's dance who came by for something to eat during the evening.

The Hotel Business Was Booming

While other parts of the country were starting to feel the effects of the stock market crash of 1929, the National Hotel seemed to be busy with guests for business and pleasure. Advertising most of Nevada County as "above the fog and below

1933 photo of the National Hotel coffee shop as it was refurbished following the November 1928 fire.

the snow belt" encouraged visitors to come. By summer of that year an upswing was underway.

In historian Gage McKinney's book *The 1930s: No Depression Here,* the author cites a short quote from *The Union* that sums up the optimistic attitude that Mr. Worth seemed to stand by: "If these be hard times, give us more hard times." [4]

A pamphlet issued in 1929 by the Hotel Greeters Club "California Hotel Guide" devoted an entire page to depicting the charms of the area.

> Picturesquely located, Nevada County is that great em-
> pire in the making, located to the northeast of Sacramento,
> forty-three miles distant when measured to its nearest
> and lowest boundary line at the Bear River Bridge on the
> Sacramento Auburn and Grass Valley Highway. An addi-
> tional stretch of sixteen entrancing miles over smoothest of
> paved scenic highways, environed by the magic of the hills
> and atmosphered with sweet smelling pines, brings you at
> a healthful and comfortable altitude of 2,500 feet to Grass
> Valley, the chief municipal entrance to Nevada County—the
> gateway to the Sierra.
>
> Here on the gentle western slope, with the golden lure of
> the West still strong and compelling lies this modest city of
> 6,000 cheerful, prosperous and hospitable souls, where, as
> in no other place of the Golden West are the days of yore so
> significantly linked with the progress for today. By way of il-
> lustration, while mines are boring and blasting into the gold
> ribbed quartz a mile below the city's surface, above soar
> birdmen of the local field of aviation, born aloft in impro-
> vised planes of local manufacture . . . . [5]

During that same summer Mr. and Mrs. Worth purchased from pioneer Louis Lutz his restaurant and lodging house on Broad Street, just below the Lace House.[6] The Lutz building, one of the oldest in the city, had been occupied by the old city hall in the early years and then by Mr. Lutz and his wife as a res-taurant and boarding house. Worth also negotiated to buy the property owed by Mrs. Samuel Clutter and others adjoining it. The Lutz property fronted forty feet on Broad Street and the Clutter property had frontage of twenty feet and extended back to Spring Street. The Worths planned to demolish the Lutz building to plant grass, flowers and shrubs. The rear of the lot was occupied by several small garages that would be repaired for use. There was no immediate plan to tear down the Clutter building, because it was in better condition— however those plans could change in the future.

In 1930 Fred Worth discovered a case in the attic of the National Hotel containing old records. Registers of the hotel dating back to 1873 were found. The 1873 volume was dusted off and brought down to be displayed on a table in the lobby. Worth thought it might be of interest to the guests and people of the town. It contained the names of old timers and guests of the hotel who were familiar to the older residents of Nevada City, and it mentioned places that were only memories. It was immediately so popular when it first went on display Worth said there was "hardly a moment of the day where there was not people looking through its pages."[7] Worth decided to have some of the interesting names and advertising found in the registers printed on sheets of blotting paper that could be inserted between the pages of the directory.

In March of 1933 it was announced that Lola Worth would retire and Fred would become the sole owner of the National.[8] It was said that continued care and responsibility for co-management of the hotel would put her health at risk. Mrs. Worth had decided to dispose of her interests in the hotel, while she planned a trip East to visit friends and relatives.

Although she planned to return later to California and there was no hint of any problems between the couple, what was left unsaid causes one to suspect there was more to the story.

Fire Visits Again and Again

The fire alarm was again sounded on July 6, 1933. This time the fire was in the two-story frame annex at the rear of the National Hotel. The fire, which took over two hours to contain, was said by firemen to be one of the most stubborn blazes to fight in recent history. Fire fighters eventually kept the fire from spreading to the main brick hotel building, but if not for the efficient and immediate response, two lives would have been lost.

By the time fire trucks arrived the building was fully engulfed. It had originated between the ceiling of the first floor and the floor of the second story in the northwest side of the annex. Nevada City fire fighters were joined by Chief Arthur Barrick and firemen from Grass Valley.

Firemen Joe O'Neill and Holden Pierce were overcome by thick smoke. O'Neill was carried unconscious from the second story by Alfred "Hopper" Eddy. His life was saved by the joint efforts of Dave Daniels (of the Empire mine first-aid crew), William C. Perry and Mrs. James Williams, a nurse who started artificial respiration. Pierce, also carried from the building, regained consciousness when he reached fresh air.

The annex housed employees of the hotel and there were a number of guest rooms on its first floor. Water from fighting the fire flowed down into the kitchen, through the coffee shop and into the office of the main hotel. Employees spent the evening mopping up and cleaning the kitchen and parts of the annex that were not burned.

Early the next morning there was no indication on the main floor of the hotel building that there had been a serious fire in the annex, and breakfast was available for early morning customers in the coffee shop.

On September 23, at 8:30 in the morning, there was great excitement (for a short time) when fire erupted in the kitchen of the National. One of the ovens in a large stove caught on fire, and when manager Mervyn Worth, son of owner Fred Worth, tried to put out the fire with an extinguisher, he was badly burned on his left hand and arm. Firemen quickly extinguished the flames and little damage was done, since the fire had been contained in the oven.

The Morning Union reported in May 1935 that an agreement had been reached following negotiations on an option to purchase the National Hotel by Charles Robinson of San Francisco. Robinson informed the paper that he had a great amount of experience in the hotel business, and if things went according to plans he would manage the hotel. Apparently these negotiations fell through, and the hotel was not sold.

Longtime owner Fred Worth died unexpectedly in Sacramento on May 3, 1938, after a short illness. When Fred

Worth's will was probated it showed he had left his estate to his sons, Mervyn D. (of Santa Cruz), Leslie S. and Fred L. (both of San Francisco), and Richard S. of Nevada City; the latter had been managing the hotel for the previous two years.

Scenes of Broad Street and the National Hotel, sometime after 1937.

16. Six Years of Transition and Confusion

RICHARD WORTH CONTINUED to manage the National until it was announced in October of 1946 that the 78-room historic hotel had been sold to George E. Murphy.[1] Murphy may have not have had enough cash to finance the purchase, for he later apparently took on several partners under the name of the National Hotel Company. Another theory is that Murphy purchased only the "business" and not the property itself. No deed has been found in Nevada County that recorded the transaction from Worth to Murphy. It is more than likely that there was a lease agreement and/or mortgage between Worth and Murphy, with an option to purchase the hotel if certain stipulations were met. It is not known when Murphy took on his additional partners, but they would be named in a foreclosure proceeding later.[2]

George Murphy, born in California and raised on the San Juan Ridge, had gained his hotel management experience by starting out as a bell hop in the St. Francis Hotel in San Francisco, and later working in hotels in Chicago and the Hawaiian Islands.[3] Murphy already owned the Shasta Springs Resort in Siskiyou County. It may have been his sister, Adelaide Murphy Jones, desk clerk at the National, who was instrumental in his decision to operate the National Hotel.

In early February 1947 George Murphy announced the hiring of Dean F. McGrath as resident manager of the National. Both Dean McGrath and his wife Laverne had served three years overseas in the U.S. Marines during the recent war. Mrs. Laverne McGrath, the daughter of Mr. and Mrs. A. H. Willard, was a graduate of the Nevada City High School class of 1939. In that same month the National Hotel Club, a cocktail lounge that had taken over the former post office space in 1946, was sold by owner John Ambler to Alton Irby.[4]

During this period of change in management there were also changes in the hotel menu. The *Nevada City Nugget* claimed

97

that old National Hotel menus were sought after by collectors.[5] At this time the history of Nevada City was added to the new menu, making it all the more appealing to guests and collectors alike.

Not quite a year after Murphy took over the National he leased the hotel to The National Hotel Company—a partnership consisting of Vance and Camile Huckins—for a term of five years with an option for two additional five-year terms.[6] Two articles appeared within a few days of each other in the *Nugget* in October 1947 that described Huckins as the new owner of the National Hotel.

Huckins was a thirty-three-year-old hotel man who said he had been in that business all his life. He owned the Clunie Hotel in Sacramento and the Gartland Hotel in San Francisco. Huckins' grandfather owned the Huckins Hotel in Oklahoma City and his father built the Drake Hotel in San Francisco. Immediately Huckins hired Floyd LeFebvre as his new manager and announced plans to renovate the hotel, starting with exterior painting. He said he would spend half his time managing the property in Nevada City. He appeared to be community-minded—or else he was just a smart businessman. Huckins told the local newspaper reporter for the *Nevada City Nugget*:

> This area should participate in the three-year [California] Centennial Celebration to the fullest. The town holds a great deal of interest for visitors. This interest should be capitalized upon, for any traveler helps nearly everyone in the community. I personally hope to be able to make a contribution to the business life of the town.[7]

Who's on First?

The next *Nugget* article appeared on February 3, 1950, announcing that Robert Ryan had purchased the hotel from "Earl Johnson and Vladimir Vucinich" of San Francisco in 1949. No assessment record or deed was recorded in Nevada County to substantiate the sale. In fact, the 1949 delinquent assessment record for Nevada County listed Richard S. and Mervyn D. Worth as the owners of the National Hotel property and George E. Murphy as their agent. The 1948 delinquent volume is missing. This further

98

suggests that Murphy purchased the hotel business or leased the property from Worth with an option to buy.

Once again the *Nevada City Nugget* carried a story of the National being sold. The story "National is Taken Over by New Owners" appeared on February 3, 1950, declaring that Leo and Ruth Weintraub of Sacramento had purchased the hotel from Robert Ryan in January and had agreed not to make changes in the hotel or dining room staff. The Weintraubs told the *Nugget* they had operated large hotels in Southern California for many years and were optimistic about the future of the hotel.[8]

Delinquent taxes from 1949 were paid by Richard S. and Mervyn D. Worth on September 20, 1950. During 1950 lawsuits were filed by various agencies in the Nevada County Superior Court against Robert Ryan, "doing business under the name of the National Hotel." Two cases were brought against Ryan by the state for unpaid business and unemployment taxes, and another was filed by the Credit Association of Grass Valley.[9]

In the middle of July Judge James Snell named banker Edwin M. Rector to take possession of the National Hotel immediately as receiver.[10] The order was issued as result of a petition by Richard Worth against George Murphy and The National Hotel Company. The petition filed by Worth stated the amount due him was $73,155.45 not yet paid from the selling price of $115,000. Worth asked for an additional five percent interest on the balance, plus $600 for an insurance payment he had advanced. Rector (a former owner of the hotel) was instructed by the court to collect all rents and profits of the hotel and hold them until further orders by the court.[11]

A decree of foreclosure was rendered by the Nevada County Superior Court on December 31, 1950, in favor of plaintiffs Richard D. Worth. Letitia Worth Haley, Mervyn Worth and Lovina Worth, and against defendants George Murphy, Curtis Vinum, William J. Greentree, Lucille Judd, Rose Margaret Murphy, The National Hotel Company—a partnership, J. Vance Huckins, Camile Vance Huckins, J. R. Ryan, Estelle G. Berglin, May W. Lemp, John Doe Johnson, Vladimir Vucinich, Milton Mizell, Leo Weintraub, First Doe, Second Doe, Third Doe, First Doe Company—a corporation, Second Doe Company—a cor-

NATIONAL HOTEL COFFEE SHOP

Nevada City, California

Sunday, July 23, 1950

DINNER MENU

———

Cream of Chicken Noodle Soup

Combination Salad   Cherry Cobbler

Ice Cream. Sherbet

———

Braised Sirloin Tips with Fresh Vegetables	90c
Fricassee of Chicken with Steamed Dumplings	$1.50
Fried Calves Liver with Bacon or Onions	$1.00
Ground Round Steak with Bordelaise Sauce	90c
Denver Omelet (3) Eggs	85c
Chicken Fried Steak, Country Gravy	$1.50
Southern Fried Chicken with Corn Fritters	$1.50
Breaded Veal Cutlets with Cream Gravy	$1.50
Roast Leg of Spring Lamb with Mint Jelly	$1.50
Roast Turkey with Celery Dressing, Cranberry Sauce	$1.75
Extra Cut Prime Ribs of Beef au jus	$1.75
Roast Leg of Pork with Dressing, Apple Sauce	$1.50
Roast Sirloin of Beef and Baked Beans	$1.25

Grilled Halibut. Lemon Butter	$1.00
Filet of Sole Tartar Sauce	95c
2 Fried Mountain Trout, Striped with Bacon	$1.50

N. Y. Cut Sirloin Steak	$2.50
Top Sirloin Steak	$2.10
Grilled Pork Chops. Apple Sauce	$1.50
Tenderloin Steak	$2.25

Creamed White Potatoes, Whole Kernel Corn

———

A LA CARTE COLD PLATES

Combination Cold Plate, Potato Salad	90c
Cold Ham. Potato Salad, Sliced Tomatoes	90c
Shrimp Salad	$1.10
Cold Sardines with Potato Salad	85c
Cottage Cheese and Fruit Salad	80c

———

Home Made Pies	15c
Ice Cold Watermelon	25c

Mr. and Mrs. Leo Weintraub, Owner-Manager.

poration, and Third Doe Company—a copartnership. As a consequence the National Hotel reverted to the Worth family. The judge ordered a sale of the property and the proceeds to be applied to the awarded Satisfaction of Judgement in the action amounting to $80,725.34 with interest and costs.[12] The National Hotel property was sold at public auction on the courthouse steps on January 27, 1951, to Richard S. Worth, Letitia Worth, Mervyn Worth and Lovina Worth for the above amount.

Richard Worth took back the management of the hotel, confident that the decade would be a good one because California was planning a three-year centennial celebration. Worth made some major changes.[13] He moved the hotel office upstairs from the ground floor to make the lobby larger and more comfortable. The ground-floor space previously occupied by the lobby was to be opened as a game room by a new tenant, Joe Powers, who had installed a taxi stand and a cigar counter in the front part of the building.

Worth refurbished many of the hotel's 70 rooms with new carpeting, wallpaper and paint. He recognized that heavy use in a busy hotel required him to purchase good quality furnishings. Canopy beds and Victorian furniture for the rooms came from England. Worth had "Mr. and Mrs." chairs especially made for the National.[14]

The remodeling downstairs created additional commercial space. In one of these spaces a new restaurant was to be opened. Its new hours would be 6:00 a.m. until 10:00 p.m. seven days a week, managed be Robert and Lettie Vroman of Grass Valley. The Vromans had extensive experience, having recently operated the dining room and kitchen of the Almanor Inn at Lake Almanor. Previously the couple managed the Tahoe Café in Grass Valley and the since-demolished hotel and restaurant in Rough and Ready. In the second space an antique shop was to be opened and operated by Mrs. Letitia Haley and Mrs. Lisetta Sheave with stock that had been gathered from the Mother Lode area along with mementoes of the Hotel.

A new museum on the second floor filled a space formerly occupied by a pair of banquet rooms. The Western museum featured California collections that Sven Skaar had been acquiring for twenty years. In the early 1940s Sven Skaar had come to Nevada City from Southern California to visit friends.[15] He and his wife eventually purchased five acres there. The following summer he took up residence in Nevada City, while his wife stayed in Southern California until she was able to quit her job as art director for a greeting card company. The couple first lived on Park Avenue in Nevada City and later built a house on North Bloomfield Road. Before moving into the hotel Skaar operated an antique store on Broad Street, and then opened the Pioneer Antique and Book shop in the old South Yuba Canal and Water Company office at 132 Main Street.[16]

At the new museum, Skaar built cubicles around the perimeter of the room and authentically reproduced an old time blacksmith shop, an old-fashioned kitchen, an assay office complete with ancient scales, as well as mineral and coin collections. His old-time bar contained a hot-water urn, a painting of a semi-nude woman, and a parade banner that used to be carried by Omega's Sons of Temperance. Skaar's country store displayed early-day pain-killers, diarrhea remedies and bed-bug poison. A children's room contained toys of the past; a miner's cabin depicted the life of an early miner. In addition to all this, he displayed a collection of guns and swords, plus the first American Flag hoisted in the Philippines during the war with Spain.

Some larger items that would not fit anywhere else were placed in the center of the museum. These included a horse-drawn hearse with brass lamps and ornaments which had been used from the 1870s until automobiles came into common use. The hearse was purchased from the Harris family in Grass Valley. Other large and interesting items included a horse cart from the long-gone Brandy City, a two-horse spring buggy—inherited by Nevada City Police Chief J. J. Jackson—which had appeared in countless Fourth of July parades, and a bell used on the first hoist of the old Empire mine in Grass Valley.

Visitors paid a small fee to visit the museum, with the profits reinvested in the purchase of additional relics for the collection.

17. Grand Opening of the National Exchange Bar

THE BAR IN THE NATIONAL HOTEL had been closed down for a three-month period until late March 1952. When the bar reopened it no longer was called the National Hotel Club, but resumed use of its historic name, National Exchange Bar. The owners, Tee and Bruce Kuehn, gave Sven Skaar complete authority in designing the bar to recreate an old-time atmosphere, while at the same time blending in the most modern conveniences. Skaar, owner of the hotel's museum, also was a talented writer and interior decorator, and he did a bang-up job. The door at the sidewalk on Broad Street led to a red rustic hallway, where on the left side was a pictorial map created by local artist Robert Gilberg, showing Nevada County with all its historic towns and local attractions.

Below the map were sectional maps and lithographs by another local artist, George Mathis. These creations had been adapted from the Skaar–Mathis "Trip Teasers" that the pair sold to tourists and locals. On the right was an exhibit of historical items from Skaar's 49er museum that included a set of gold scales. Inside the bar room many objects were mounted on high shelves against a background of newly painted cool green walls. The items displayed were from the 1890s or earlier.

Skaar installed an elaborately carved mahogany sideboard from the Claus Spreckles mansion on San Francisco's Van Ness Avenue. Antique chandeliers, mining equipment, rare early prints, and lithographs and paintings adorned the room to create an atmosphere in which anyone, "the logger, the businessman, the miner and the scholar," could feel comfortable. A grand opening lasting all day and evening was held on April 3, 1952, with hors d'oeuvres served at the cocktail hour and music for dancing provided by Arch Brooks and his Rhythm Ramblers.

The remodeling work that was taking place on the ground floor of the National during the first two months of 1953 was

The National Exchange Bar in the 1950s.

The National bar as it looks today.

kept under wraps until nearly the end of February, when all was revealed. Tom Stevens of Oakland had purchased the National Hotel coffee shop on February first and now he closed the deal to buy the National Exchange Bar from Bruce Kuehn. Stevens already owned Ramsey's Café on Broad Street. He had remodeled the former National lobby into a steak restaurant that was served from the former coffee-shop kitchen (which explains the existing door between the dining room and bar). Stevens said the doorway to the restaurant would be closed for privacy when there were parties of diners. The new restaurant was only open for dinners and late dining, but luncheon groups could use the dining room at noon. The first group to utilize the new facility was the Nevada City Soroptimist Club, which did so before the official opening, reserving the room for forty members.

The summer of 1953 brought chuck-wagon-style dining to the National's new Saddle and Sirloin restaurant. Beginning in August Tom Stevens offered "a traditional western eating plan which dates to Pioneer times." He would give the customers "a lusty eating plan in which the diner gets all he wants and second helpings."[1] Although not on the scale of today's all-you-can-eat buffets, this 1950s version offered the choice of two entrees and an "assortment of the usual trimmings." In the 1950s, restaurants that offered extra servings were very popular. Two such were the Trails End and Club Martini in San Francisco. To introduce the new eating plan, Stevens opened with a "Western Night." A dance orchestra was hired, and customers dressed in the best Western outfits received prizes.

Sven Skaar, proprietor of the National's 49er museum, was named acting-president of the Nevada County Historical Society in October 1955, replacing M. Henry Argall, the Grass Valley newspaperman who died of a heart attack that month. Skaar had been serving as vice president of the organization during the previous year.

The directors of the Nevada County Historical Society received a request from the Nevada County Board of Trade to outline the important facts about the county's history and earliest residents, following an inquiry from a motion picture company who had an interest in the Donner Party. The directors of the

historical society voted to help the project by making tape re-
cordings of stories by older citizens who could recall handed-
down stories of the past. Skaar noted that there were only one
or two Indians left in the area who were still able to speak the
language of the local Indians. If their language was not recorded
it could be lost forever.

After moving out of its space on Number 1 Winter Street, the
Nevada City office of the state Board of Equalization moved into
a street-floor office of the National Hotel building on September
18, 1958. L. H. "Bill" Wilson, the district tax administrator in
Marysville, explained that a location in the downtown business
section of Nevada City at the National Hotel would better serve
the public. The office served a large geographic area, provid-
ing individual tax assistance for towns as far as 160 miles away.
Besides Nevada County, it also served most of Sierra County,
Squaw Valley, the north side of Lake Tahoe in Placer County and
the cities of Reno, Sparks and Fallon in Nevada. In addition, the
Nevada City office handled the collection of sales, use tax, transportation tax and diesel fuel taxes for the City of Nevada, the
City of Grass Valley and the County of Nevada.

Sven Skaar's Western Museum in the National Hotel.

18. The Mod Sixties and the Issue that Literally Split Nevada City

DURING THE 1960s much of the information written in newspapers and magazines about the National Hotel was erroneous. This decade was far removed from the early years and reminiscences of pioneers who had witnessed events in Nevada City's early history. For anyone in the 1960s researching the original records there was not yet a local history branch library such as we have today, with cabinets containing hundreds of files about Nevada County's past—including information on pioneers and early settlers, towns, organizations, buildings and local events.

The Searls Historical Library, owned and operated by the Nevada County Historical Society, would be established a decade later to preserve and make available thousands of index cards citing articles, letters, diaries, books and photos and other miscellaneous papers and records that were be sorted, indexed, cataloged and kept for future generations to research.

In the 1960s the local newspapers had yet not been indexed. Although over 100 years of local newspapers were mostly intact, there were few search aids available to make researching quicker or easier. One had to read each issue of a newspaper line by line and day by day. It was easier for some writers and reporters who came to town simply to accept any tradition or story shared by a local who seemed to be knowledgeable about the National's long history. (And it has been said that this often was done while sharing a drink or two at the National Hotel's bar.)

Previous articles about the National were used as historic references. Unfortunately, erroneous facts and dates would be reprinted in newly written articles. At the beginning of his term, Marvin Haddy, the 1960 president of the Nevada City Chamber of Commerce, used the occasion of a chamber dinner at the National Hotel to predict that a "boom" was on the horizon. It happened that Haddy lived in Grass Valley. The newly elected Grass Valley Chamber president, Scott Barrow, lived in Nevada

City, and Haddy predicted that there would be "good cooperation between the twin cities" that year.[1]

One of the chamber's goals was to clean up Deer Creek at the downtown Plaza. The creek, which had been overrun by thousands of miners in the early days, was said to be in a disgraceful condition. Tourists passing through who might otherwise stop and "spend a few dollars" were being repelled by the mess, it was said. Dick Worth, owner of the National Hotel, was on the newly elected slate of officers for that year, along with Florence Kendrick, the first woman anyone could recall being on the board of directors.

In order to make the community a better place to live, the board listed as its main goals the desire to make improvements in transportation, water, sanitation and parking. They determined to take a more active part in local government and would seek to reach their goals by "cashing in on historical values in the community, and forgetting petty differences."[2]

The decade of the 1960s is remembered for the important decisions that were made that altered the character of Nevada City right up to the present day. The Gold Rush town that sprang up almost overnight in the 1850s would, little by little, re-invent itself in the 1960s and become a charming and widely-admired example of Gold Rush/Victorian community planning and a highly popular California tourist destination.

The Golden Center Freeway

Two issues that would affect everyone in Nevada City would not be finally settled until near the end of the decade. One had to do with creation of an historical ordinance (see Chapter 20), and the other involved a freeway plan that—both figuratively and literally—split the historic Gold Rush town. Originally called the Gold Run Freeway, and later named the Golden Center Freeway, this highway proposal destroyed friendships and nearly wrecked the town.

The original freeway plan had been adopted by the state in 1951, after three years of study from 1948–1951. It might have been built years earlier had not another highway construction project been given preference. When the Olympic Winter Games necessitated widening U.S. Highway 40 to four lanes, this delayed the Nevada County plan.

The proposed freeway construction had been justified originally due to the supposedly heavy levels of traffic between and through Grass Valley and Nevada City. In hindsight this seems laughable at best, when compared with today's traffic jams. But in those days there was money to spare for such projects, and state officials were determined to build them.

The existing routes of highways 20 and 49 brought traffic through the heart of Nevada City, which was a nuisance for some, but a welcome feature for those who catered to travelers and tourists—such as hotels, restaurants, gas stations and antique stores. There was only one route through Nevada City for truck traffic, and authorities quoted statistics that predicted area traffic increase exponentially in coming years, just as was happening throughout California and across the nation.

Since the city council did not have funds in its coffers to improve or widen the streets, it was argued that the proposed freeway would provide at least "one modern street going the length of the city." The freeway opponents called it "Calamity Cut," and with the hindsight of later sensitivity to (and interest in) historic and ecological preservation, a 1980 magazine article described the freeway as:

> . . . an affront to principles of enlightened highway planning. It is ironic that since the state legislature recommended that Highway 49 be designated a state scenic highway in 1963, the California Department of Transportation (CalTrans) has irrevocably destroyed many significant resources within that corridor. The most dramatic effect of the freeway in Nevada City is the barrier it creates to east-west access across Nevada City as Broad and Main streets entered from the west and Boulder and Sacramento streets from the east and south. Main street, south of Union Street, was eliminated and access to the plaza was cut off. The Union Hotel, the Union and National livery and feed stables, several saloons, hardware stores, and an undertaker's office formerly occupied the portions of Main and Broad streets eliminated by the freeway.[3]

After a special meeting in county supervisor's chambers on October 4, 1960, the situation as it stood was put in simple terms, that the freeway as planned be accepted—or nothing would be built for a long time. Attending were State Senator Ron Cameron, Assemblyman Paul Lunardi, California Division of Highway officials, local government officials and invited interested individuals.

At that meeting the proposed route of the freeway was shown. It would enter the city's south limits near the site of the Angelini garage, cross Deer Creek in a "low slow arc" and proceed up the north bank, passing under Broad Street just south of the National Hotel, cross Main Street at Ott's Assay office and then proceed north, parallel to Coyote Street, in the stream bed that drains the Manzanita diggings.[4]

Slogans like "concrete or cobwebs," sprang up predicting that if the freeway were to go around the city entirely and leave the city intact, motorists most likely would bypass the city, since it would be inconvenient to stop. They would visit and spend their tourist dollars in other more accessible towns instead. Marv Haddy, the chamber of commerce president, brought up the sure loss of tourist dollars if the freeway did not enter Nevada City, because "Nevada City derives much economic value from tourist trade—not necessarily the picture-takers and painters, but the recreationist–vacationist who uses Nevada City to stock up before taking off for the upper country."[5]

Many expressed dread that a "concrete monster" would replace and intrude upon the present "peaceful landscape," destroying quaint picture-taking allure. There was no lack of concern from community members, business people, and government officials both at the local and state level. Although it was generally agreed by the majority of people that a freeway was needed and wanted, the proposed route was questioned— and a main concern was a loss of historic buildings.

One of the most prominent historic places was the site of Ott's Assay Office. After the 1863 fire had burned his original wooden building, J. J. Ott had moved next door into a brick building constructed in 1855 that had survived the 1856 fire. There Ott had processed much of the gold mined locally, and is famous for having assayed and weighed the first ore taken from the Comstock Lode in what later became the state of Nevada.

The ore samples were brought to Nevada City by horseback in June of 1859 by former residents of Nevada County, J. F. Stone and W. P. Morrison, who had purchased an interest in the lode discovered by Henry T. P. Comstock.[6] When Ott's assay confirmed the richness of the ore, it resulted in a silver rush to that place and it is said that it emptied the town of Nevada for a time. Gradually men who had gone to the Comstock, but did not strike it rich, came back to Nevada City, while others who stayed in Virginia City opened businesses instead of mining for silver.

A second historic building of concern to Nevada City residents was the South Yuba Canal Office next door to Ott's building. Originally the Potter building, it (like its neighbor) was made of brick and was one of the few that survived the 1856 fire. After 1861 it became the headquarters for the largest network of water flumes and ditches in the state. Its early engineers built a 16-mile canal (including a 3,200 foot tunnel) at a cost of $350,000. That system provided a practically inexhaustible supply of water to the town and nearby mines.

One suggestion was that the state could sell the Ott building to the City of Nevada at a very low price, and then deed to the city the state-owned park on Union Street, after leveling and preparing it as a site to which the assay office could be moved. Part of the park area itself was of historic significance as the site of the

> . . . first building on Broad Street and second to be erected within the present bounds of Nevada City Township. A log cabin had been built there in September 1849 by John Truesdale, a prominent merchant. The cabin once stood in the clearing now occupied by the present park, on the lot where the Alpha Hardware building now is and overlooked the little flat now bisected by Main Street . . . [7]

That log cabin was thought to be the first permanent building in Nevada City.

However, local residents were informed that neither federal nor state funds were available to move the brick Ott structure, since neither the United States nor California governments considered the building "of sufficient historical value." The proposed moving would have to be funded by the city or by local donations. In the end, both the Ott and South Yuba Canal buildings were saved by an adjustment made to the freeway. Eight years later, shortly after the freeway was completed, both buildings would fall within the district created in 1968 by Nevada City's Historic Ordinance,. Over the next few decades that ordinance would alter the town's appeal more than any short-term effects brought about by the freeway.

The South Yuba Canal Office was registered as a California Historical Landmark in 1970 (No. 832) and the Original Ott Assay Office Site was designated a National Historic Landmark on April 4, 1975, with a plaque placed on May 16, 1975, by the Nevada County Historical Landmarks Commission.

Another landmark that was of concern was the giant Sequoia tree which stood in the front of Bergemann's Funeral Home on Sacramento Street. The tree, planted in 1863 by early pioneers, had become a community Christmas tree, and when decorated with lights was visible all over town.[8] The tree was not spared, and in 1965 was removed. After the tree was taken down it was milled for lumber from which park benches and tables were constructed by members of E Clampus Vitus Chapter 10 for the Clampicnic Area of Malakoff Diggins State Historic Park.

Nevada County's district attorney, who had arranged the October 1960 meeting to try to work out the freeway concerns, called upon various people to speak and explained that those present represented a cross-section of Nevada City sentiment. Those who spoke on the "purported loss of aesthetic values" were Harold Berliner, Alf Heller, Dean Thompson, Bob Paine, Jack Brickell, Elza Kilroy, and Ed Uren.

The next day the Nevada City Planning Commission announced they wanted no part of the freeway controversy. At the meeting the previous night, two motions made by Elza Kilroy failed to pass. One was that the city council hold an election on the issue. The other was to adopt a recommendation to the city council that they give consideration to an alternate route through the city. Since there was a lack of support, both motions were withdrawn.[9]

The next week the Nevada City Council requested that the state division of highways provide maps and data regarding the proposed route of the freeway through Nevada City and the three alternate routes that had been surveyed over a number of years. The map was displayed in City Hall for the public to view, along with data that explained the economic factors. Colored tape was placed along each route to make it very clear and easy for the public to understand. The route which the freeway follows today was designated Route A and was the one approved by both the planning commission and the city council years ago. Plan A would take out 30 businesses (of which 16 had already been purchased) and 35 residences (of which 19 had been purchased).

Route D ran east of the city center and followed a line northwest from Gold Flat along Nimrod Street (west of Pioneer Park), crossed Boulder Street at the home of Mrs. J. B. Christie (the historic Martin Luther Marsh House), crossed Willow Valley road east of Aristocracy Hill and west of the old Nevada County Hospital, and continued east to intersect with Highway 20. A cutoff would be built along Aristocracy Hill to intersect with Highway 49 near North Bloomfield Road. Route D, the next most direct route through town was 3.3 mile in length, with a difference in length of 0.4 miles; it would have taken out three businesses and 70 residences.

Two routes, B and C, had little difference between them. Both would travel in a westerly circle around the town to intersect with Highway 49 beyond the terminus of West Broad Street. Route B would run 3.4 miles, and turn west from the intersection of Lower Grass Valley and Gold Flat roads, run through the State Forestry headquarters, across the end of Brock Road and proceed northwest along the city limits. It would need right-of-way through four businesses and four residential properties, and take out 8 businesses and 50 residences.

Route C would turn west at Town Talk and cut across Ridge Road, through the State Forestry ground west to B, cross Brock Road and follow much the same route as Route B to the intersection with 49. It was 3.3 miles long and would eliminate four businesses and 35 houses. The only point in favor of these routes was that each almost completely by-passed the city.

Mrs. Jean Worth, co-owner of the National Hotel, was concerned that the hotel annex would have to go, and without the annex the hotel could not operate profitably. "If the hotel means anything to the city at all," she said, "then the city should adopt either Plan C or the DeLeuw, Cather plan."[10] She was referring to a plan drawn up by the firm of DeLeuw, Cather and Company of San Francisco, which had been prepared under the direction of engineer Robert Conradt. The engineering firm had been hired to come up with a proposal that would "blend the state's desires for engineering feasibility with the city's desires for true scenic qualities."[11] Both Mrs. Worth and Dick Keen supported Plan C.

Near the end of October a joint announcement was made by Dick Knee and Bob Paine that residents and property owners would have an opportunity to cast a plebiscite on the Nevada City freeway route on Tuesday, November 22. Sample ballots would be mailed to every Nevada City registered voter, and property owners who lived out of town would also be permitted to vote. Each sample ballot carried a paragraph by Paine and his supporters offering reasons to bypass the business district of Nevada City. Donations were collected by both sides to pay for the cost of the election.

An advertisement that appeared in *The Union* urging citizens to vote for the bypass route listed the names of residents who supported that issue. Long editorials also appeared in the newspaper over the next few weeks up until the day before the election, telling voters that the " . . . proposed route was adopted after long and careful planning by the California Highway Commission. . . . There was no thought of another route until the past year when a very determined propaganda campaign was started by a small number of people for purposes best known to themselves, but obviously the dominant purpose was publicity."[12]

When all was said and done, the *Union* editorial which appeared the day before the election summed up a battle that had been forged by public controversy and opposition for eight months: " . . . the unofficial, public opinion poll would be that; only an opinion poll with no legal standing, backing or implications as far as any public or governmental agency was concerned and would not be binding."[13]

114

The day before the election an editorial in *The Union* stated that many people who were concerned with the freeway issue would not be able to cast their votes. These were people who lived in Nevada City, supported the economy, but who worked out-of-town and would not be able to get back in time to cast their votes before the polling place was closed. Others, who lived outside the city limits but had interests in the town and spent their money in Nevada City, were not allowed to cast a vote. Probably due to the editorial in the newspaper, it was decided at the last minute that people who had businesses in the city but lived outside of the city limits could cast their votes.

The voting day came and went, and the votes were counted. A large majority voted in favor of building the freeway in the downtown location along the route proposed by the state. Of the 541 votes cast, 333 voted to by-pass the city. After the votes had been counted Mayor Carr said

> Now that the people have given the city council a very clear mandate it only remains for all the people to unite behind a drive to get this freeway built at the earliest pos-

We, the undersigned, strongly urge our fellow citizens of Nevada City to

VOTE FOR THE
BYPASS
ROUTE

In the Special Freeway Election,
Tuesday, November 22, 1960

Mrs. Mary Warnecke	Miss Emmaline Andersen
Miss Savory Ford	Elza Kilroy
John Sballi	Violet Chapman
Bradley Legg	Mrs. C. S. Haley
Mrs. Arthur Innes	Albert Johnson
Lloyd Penrose	Mr. and Mrs H. M. Haley
Mrs. George W. Downey	Mr. and Mrs. Stan Jones
Mrs. Ernest F. Buck	Mrs. E. M. Rector
V. and Mrs. E. Shaw	Evelyn Corr
Reiha Downey	Mr. and Mrs. Guy E.
Mrs. J. B. Christie	Smith
M. and Mrs. Al Wallis	David Osborn
Mrs. L. L. Myers	Madeline Draper
Charles Woods	Mrs. Gladys Ohme
Charles Parsons	Grace Keenan
I. F. Davis	Maude Keenan
Helen Bontecou	Mr. and Mrs. Douglas
Mrs. H. W. Robinson	Farmer
Robert Gilberg	Mrs. Georgina O'Connor
Mr. and Mrs. Carl Libby	Miss Alma Marsh
Dorothy Waggoner	Mr. and Mrs. Robert Fetz
Mr. and Mrs. R. Chesney	Mr. and Mrs. Otis
Mr. and Mrs. Stan Hall	Gaylord
Dr. and Mrs. McPherson	Mr. and Mrs. Robert
Mr. and Mrs. Sven Skaar	Paine
Mr. and Mrs. R. McMasters	Mr. and Mr. Clayton
	Bennett
Mr. De Martini	Father M McClusky
Mr. and Mrs. Pert	Kay Zwenchek
Al Shaley	Mrs. Charlotte Beemer
F. C. Uren	John Webster
Mrs. Horatio L. Small	Mr. and Mrs. Miles
	Coughlin

WE CAN'T AFFORD A
DIVIDED TOWN

sible time. With a united community we should be able to expedite the matter. It is time to quit bickering and work together for the good of the city.[15]

The newly adopted revised plan saved the National Hotel Annex, as well as the Ott's Assay Office and the South Yuba Canal Office, by construction of a retaining wall. The freeway construction did not begin until 1965. In the next few years *The Nugget* newspaper printed a special edition each August called the *Progress Edition*. It reported changes in the county, and kept the public informed about the many different projects in business, school and home construction, up-to-date economic news, as well as recreational development and activity around the county. The civil leaders and state highway department obviously had many phone calls and letters inquiring about the delay in beginning work on the freeway.

This aerial view of freeway construction shows Coyote Street left of center, in front of St. Canice Catholic Church.

By the mid-summer of 1964 the conversion of old U.S. 40 to an interstate highway was almost complete. The contractor had estimated that it would be completed on October first. W. L. Warren, district engineer for the eleven-county Highway District 3 announced that there were two state highway projects set to start in the near future. The most important was the long await-ed freeway, now morphed into Interstate 80 most of the way, which could not be begun until after the U.S. 40 was finished. It was expected that the first part of the Grass Valley-Nevada City freeway, three-mile section running from Brunswick Road east to Nevada City would go to bid in September and was expected to cost about $4 million. The other project was expected to be-gin the next month. It was the improvement of the intersection of State Route 20 and Alta Ridge Road about 1½ miles west of Grass Valley.

The Golden Center Freeway was dedicated and opened on December 17, 1969, twenty-five years after it was conceived. Done in Gold Country style, Mrs. Lita Brockington Shanly burned the traditional golden ribbon with a carbide mining lamp upon the site of the Golden Center Mine in Grass Valley. Mrs. Shanly's father, Charles Brockington, retired as superintendent of the large-producing mine that grew out of her mother's sug-gestion that they form a company to mine the veins they knew existed in the their own backyard.[15]

What we take for granted today seemed very odd in the 1960s: the idea that two Nevada County highways would be included in preliminary plans for a state scenic highway. Both highways 20 and 49 were chosen to be part of the scenic high-way system—5,000 miles of roads chosen for special attention because of their outstanding natural beauty.

19. Hundred-Year Club and a Swimming Pool

BACK IN 1948 the 100-Year Club was founded in California for the purpose of recognizing families, businesses and special agricultural interests that had been maintained for at least a century. Today the organization is the California Agricultural Heritage Club and the focus is on agribusiness or agriculturally related businesses. (Special recognition was added in 2001 for those who had continued their operations 125 and 150 years; in 2010 special recognition given to those who completed 175 years.) Each year there is a special ceremony at the state fair to honor new members. In 1960 there were 267 members from all areas of business, industry and agriculture.

In September 1960 the National Hotel became one of only three businesses in Nevada County to qualify for the 100-Year Club. That year Lieutenant Governor Glen Anderson presented a plaque and medallion to Bob and Ruth Paine of Nevada City at an Admission Day luncheon. The Paines were representing the hotel's owners, Dick and Jean Worth. Two county businesses that had joined the club previously were Grass Valley Hardware (in 1954) and the Holbrooke Hotel (in 1951). Later, in 1964, the *Union* newspaper was added to the membership.

It is this writer's opinion that the National Hotel—entered for the year 1954—ought to have been entered in 1956, a hundred years after it first opened. Likewise, The Holbrooke should have been honored later than it was. The Holbrooke Hotel did not operate continuously from 1851, for it was the Exchange Hotel after the 1855 Grass Valley fire, and its name was changed at least three times during its existence. On August 6, 1918, the Holbrooke became the Grass Valley Hotel and a news story declared, "the Holbrook [sic] was no more."[1]

It was early November of 1960 when the management of the National installed the "ultra-modern" concrete swimming pool in back of the hotel lobby, and the area west of the rear annex

The modern swimming pool behind the National as it was in the 1960s.

was cleared and paved for parking spaces for hotel guests.

Accompanying the news of the swimming pool was an historical article by historian H. P. Davis that appeared in the *Nevada City Nugget* along with a photo of the pool at the National. Like other writers of the era, Davis could be counted upon to add a flourish to whatever he wrote:

> For more than sixty million years the native granite from which this pool was excavated, had remained undisturbed by the hand of man. In the spring of 1851, a hundred and nine years ago, this site was the scene of an event of significance in the early history of the town and county. Here was convened a Committee of Public Safety for the purpose of apprehending and punishing three malefactors charged with stealing $2,600 in gold from a merchant of this community.

> To appreciated the full significance of this trial, it must be realized that this little settlement, then known as "Nevada" and soon to be incorporated as the "City of Nevada," had been in existence only about fifteen months, and further, one must realize that the area in which it was then located was yet within the boundary of Yuba County.

When created, Yuba County embraced all of the area of Yuba, Nevada and Sierra counties and a part of Placer County. Marysville, on the Feather River, at the head of deep water navigation, was chosen as the county seat. . . . By the spring of 1851 placer gold had been found in every large river and in innumerable ravines and seasonable water courses on the western slope of the Sierra Nevada, from the Feather River to the Tuolumne, a distance of more than one hundred and fifty miles.[2]

Back Luck and Plenty Tourism

In October of 1960 a house behind the National Hotel at Spring Street and the intersection of National Alley was sold to the state to be demolished and the site cleared. It was one of three parcels sold that month to make room for the coming freeway, two of which were in Grass Valley. The Nevada City building was once the infamous brothel that inspired complaints by hotel guests and nearby residents, who suggested it was "not always used for strictly residential purposes"; it was the same house that Mayor Rector had objected to at city trustees meeting decades earlier.[3]

A fire alarm on the afternoon of December 10, 1960, brought fire trucks from Nevada City and Grass Valley companies to Broad Street, right below the National Hotel Alley. A fire had started at the Prentiss photography studio located in the bottom floor of the wooden hotel annex.[4] Even though the fire was quickly brought under control, the photography studio was almost totally destroyed, and the studio of Mathis, Woods and Osborn next door was badly damaged by water and smoke.[5] The rooms above the annex suffered some smoke damage, but they would still be usable.

It was learned later that Lincoln Abrahamson, one of the partners at Prentiss studio, had gone out for lunch and left an electric heater running. That may have overloaded equipment or caused a short circuit; in any case, chemicals in the studio were most likely responsible for spreading the fire so quickly. All that was left was charred wood and mangled metal—the loss of equipment and supplies amounted to $3,000. Luckily, the studio owners, Robert Wyckoff and E. Lincoln Abrahamson Jr., who

The Prentiss photography studio appears at the far left in this photo of the National Annex, Alley, Coffee Shop and Hotel.

had operated the business for only one month, had increased their fire insurance policy a week before the fire.

Most disappointed were the families who had recently taken their children to the studio for Christmas portraits. The happy, smiling faces of children that had been captured by the camera only days and weeks before, could not be printed or picked up by parents to be given to family and friends, since all the negatives and prints in the studio were lost in the fire.

A *Nugget* article several days after the fire declared, "Its future fate already sealed by the recent city vote endorsing a downtown freeway route . . . the National Hotel Annex will be boarded up to await the day of destruction for the future Nevada City freeway." [6] When the *Sunset Northern California Travel Guide* was published in 1960, Grass Valley and Nevada City were featured in the section on the Northern Mines. This publication

ALL OUR WATER IS CLEARIFIED

APPETIZERS

Crab or Shrimp Cocktail . . .	1.00
Marinated Herring	.75
Assorted Relish for Two . . .	.75
Fruit Cocktail	.50
Chilled Tomato Juice	.35

SOUPS & SALADS

Soup Du Jour . .35 Bowl . .50	
Tossed Green Dinner Salad . . .50	
Hearts of Lettuce 50	
Combination Vegetable Salad . . 1.75	
Chef's Salad 2.00	
Crab or Shrimp Louie 2.50	

Dressings: Oil and Vinegar, Roquefort, French or 1000 Island

VICTORIAN DELUXE DINNERS

Assorted Relishes   Soup Du Jour   Chef's Tossed Green Salad   Choice of Dressing

CHOICE OF ENTREES

CHOICE PRIME RIBS OF BEEF, FRIDAY, SATURDAY AND SUNDAY ONLY . .	3.95
Breaded Veal ala Marsala	2.50
Chicken Fried Steak	2.50
Chicken Livers Sauted in Wine, Mushrooms with Rice	3.25
Beef Brochette Served on a Bed of Rice	3.50
Grenadine of Beef Tenderloin au Burgundy, with Noodles	3.50
Sauerbraten German Style	3.50
Pork Chops, Broiled or Breaded, Mushroom Sauce	3.95
Beef Stroganoff	3.75
Tournedos of Beef ala Bernaise.	3.95
Charcoal Broiled Dinner Steak	3.75
Charcoal Broiled Top Sirloin	4.50
Charcoal Broiled New York Cut	4.95
Charcoal Broiled Filet Mignon	5.25
Charcoal Broiled Lamb Chops	4.95
Scallops, Breaded and Deep Fried, with Tartar Sauce	2.50
Filet of Sole Grilled in Butter with Tarter Sauce	2.50
Halibut Steak, Grilled or broiled, Lemon Butter, Tartar Sauce	2.50
Swordfish Steak, Broiled or Baked, Lemon Butter, Tarter Sauce	2.75
Stuffed Eastern Shrimp	2.95
Breaded Eastern Oysters	2.95
Broiled Lobster, Parsley Butter	3.95
Lobster Thermidor	4.45
Broiled Lobster Tails	4.95
Chateaubriand for Two . . . . Per Person	6.25
Filet de Boeut Roti (Roast Filet of Beef) . . . . Per Person	6.25

Choice of Baked, or French Fried Potatoes

Coffee, Tea or Milk	Fresh Vegetables	Hot Breads

Entrees 50c Less on Ala Carte

Victorian dining room menu from the 1960s found on e-Bay by the author.

was revised and republished over next several decades and became a standard publication for travel in Northern California.

In 1962 a magazine article that appeared in *Sunset* magazine was responsible for a great many of the tourists who came to Nevada City—and to the National Hotel in particular—throughout the rest of the decade. Whenever reservations could not be obtained at the height of tourist season, potential guests would book them for the next season. The influx of tourists had begun in August of 1961 when the travel news editor for *Sunset*, Frances Colebend, spent several days in Nevada City, where she talked to civic leaders and historians. She visited old cemeteries, museums and private homes, gathering material and photos for her upcoming piece. The article would show every season in Nevada City, and photo teams had been sent to Nevada City to take color photographs. The *Sunset* writer called Nevada City "one of the most beautiful of all Sierra hill towns."[7]

A big event was held on Sunday, May 5, 1963, in Nevada City honoring the National Hotel. Three hundred members of William Bull Meek–William Morris Stewart Chapter 10, E Clampus Vitus, led by Noble Grand Humbug Herb Gerrish, dedicated a bronze plaque on the outside wall of the National Hotel to commemorate the historic importance of the hotel to Nevada City and the community. *The Union* carried an article prior to the event, which read in part:

> A National Exchange Hotel was erected in 1849 and has been continuously operated as a hotel since that time. Other hotels in California were erected at an earlier date but none have continued to serve the public in the same capacity as the National . . . . [8]

It is surprising that no one from the community or the historical society came forward to correct that erroneous date or the fact that no rustic wood hotel built in 1849 had any connection to the present-day hotel building. The fact is, the brick building originally known as the Bicknell block (which the National still occupies) was not completed until April 1856.

20. Historical District Established

BESIDES THE FREEWAY CONTROVERSY, the second major issue in the late 1960s that would affect Nevada City's future was historical in nature. After the Nevada City Planning Commission recommended to the city council that a recently studied historical zoning plan be made into an ordinance, it was passed unanimously. Adopted on August 12, 1968, the ordinance went into effect 30 days later. It called for the "preservation of such places and buildings, and of the architectural appearance of the surrounding properties within the historical district, being essential to the economic and cultural life of the city." [1]

Buildings included in the ordinance as being "symbolic of the city's historical past as a mining town during the days of the California Gold Rush and thereafter" were Ott's assay office, the Nevada City Methodist Church, Trinity Episcopal Church, St. Canice Catholic Church, Community Baptist Church, the New York Hotel, the *Nugget* building, the *Union* building, the Osborn and Woods store, the Chinese laundry, the National Hotel, Firehouses 1 and 2, the Nevada Opera House, Masonic Temple and the Searls law office.

The ordinance stated that exteriors of buildings within the historical zone should be not altered unless the change fell within the architectural category referred to in the ordinance as "Mother Lode" style. This style was defined as having tall narrow windows, iron or wood shutters and constructed of wood, brick or stone.

All signs installed after the ordinance went into effect must comply with its restrictions—and the ordinance required the planning commission to approve all projects proposed within the historical zone before building permits could be issued.

In addition, the city had agreed to continued cooperation with Nevada County's "Overall Economic Development Plan" for future growth and prosperity.

This photo, taken from the back of National Alley facing Broad Street, shows the glassed-in overhead walkway connecting the National Hotel to its wooden annex on the right.

The National Annex Is No More

It was two weeks later, in August 1968, eight years after the fire that destroyed two studios in the National Hotel Annex, that the building was taken down to make room for the freeway. The building had been declared unsafe ever since the fire in 1960. The back section of the annex had once served as a clothing store, probably as early as 1897. In one section was an area known as the "pattern room," where former employees had written their signatures on what over time had become a "roster," or a "mini-hall of fame."

On August 11, 1897, Bert Chegwidden had placed his signature on the wall (Chegwidden later became the owner of Bert's Dry Goods Store in Grass Valley). Some, whose signatures appear in faded ink, were H. L. "Babe" Childers, Sam Hooper, and Lloyd Penrose. Sam H. Hooper's name was written in 1934 and Childers' on April 1, 1941, with a notation by the signer that it was "all fools day."

These three men were still a part of the community and active on Broad Street in 1968 when the annex was demolished: Hooper was the city clerk; Childers and Penrose were employed at Novak's Clothing Store, where Babe was the manager. Reminiscing later, the three businessmen recalled a time when a clothing store in the back of the annex was called The Lace House, with S. Lee Leiter the one-time owner. After he sold his interest, it was divided into men's and women's departments under separate management, with William Holm operating the men's store and young Babe Childers as his employee.

Other names on the "roster" that were not dated were those of George Fortier, Billy Hanks, Miss Parker, Ruby Walker, Kathy Shier, Bertha Majors, Gladys Clemo, Mayme Solari and Mamie Grimes.

A story in the local newspaper in September 1969 featured the National as the "Great Grandpappy of Elegantly-restored Hotels." Once again the National was incorrectly credited with operating "continuously since 1854." [2]

Dick and Jean Worth sold the National Hotel to Dick and Nan Ness in September 1972. An appreciation dinner sponsored by the Nevada City Chamber of Commerce was held at the National

Hotel for Dick Worth, and an article in the local newspaper contained the erroneous statement that Dr. Bicknell had built the "commodious and strictly fireproof complex in 1854."[3] No doubt this information was borrowed from previous stories published in the 1950s and 60s.

The article also repeated a long-held misconception about when the National's new balcony was built. Its construction was completed by March 1894, as evidenced by newspaper ads using an engraving of the National with a large balcony on the front. (Older drawings showed a narrow decorative railing.) The wedding of Vivie Alice Rector and Iraneus Cory Lindley took place on June 27, 1900, and John Mott Rector's historical narration, *Eleven Generations of the Rector Family,* states that "a large wedding reception was held on the wide, newly built veranda of the hotel, which had just been completed in time for the occasion." Perhaps the balcony was remodeled prior to the wedding, but the 1894 view looks very much the same as today.

Before the freeway was built, the National Hotel gazebo was

September 1974 Constitution Day Parade on Broad Street, before a new ordinance required replacement of existing signs.

The gazebo that was removed from the National Annex was reattached to a back building on the hotel property.

located prominently on the glass-walled bridge (walkway) between the National's main building and the wooden annex on the other side of the National Alley. Today that property is a paved parking lot above the freeway on-ramp. After the gazebo was taken down, it had been moved around the property for several years. In March 1973 it was placed between two little buildings behind the National, where it could be easily seen from the freeway. Owner Jack Ness and his wife announced that they would paint the gazebo gold with "gingerbread trim" and attach a new weather vane to replace the old one, reproducing it as closely as possible.

Dick Ness, with the help of Hugh Brodie and Tom Moss, removed the old National Hotel sign that projected out and over Broad Street at the front entrance. He also removed other signs to conform to the newly adopted Nevada City Historic District Ordinance. By a vote of the city council, a newly located bus stop on lower Broad Street in front of the National warranted a new post and sign to be erected on the wooden sidewalk.[4] Later that year a room known as the Gold Dining Room (first door above National Alley) was remodeled and became the new office of Placer Savings and Loan.

Bus loads of movie crews and actors from Hollywood—including actress Ann Baxter as a guest star—arrived at the National in 1974. It was the cast of "Cannon," a popular television detective series that ran from 1971–1976, starring William Conrad. Ann Baxter was to have the "best room in the house," which was the bridal suite. Unfortunately, the hotel had not received this request in advance, and the hitch was that the suite was already reserved for a newly married couple who were yet to arrive. Baxter thoughtfully gave the room up to the newlyweds.[5]

The Bicentennial Celebration

There were plenty of opportunities in 1976, the Nation's Bicentennial, for more erroneous historical facts to be republished, and reporters and publicists did not disappoint the critics. One of the worst, containing what might be called "fractured facts," was published in January 1976, entitled, "A literal gold mine? National Hotel moves into its 122nd year."[6]

The reporter obviously relied on earlier magazine stories as references, and failed to conduct any primary research. Had he consulted the popular standard reference, *1880 History of Nevada County, California,* he would not have written:

> The National Hotel is today the oldest continuously operating hotel west of the Rockies . . . a major Nevada City attraction for 122 years now, the National began as four buildings in 1851. Three years later it was turned into a hotel and has been going strong ever since . . . remaining in the hands of just four families.[7]

THE NATIONAL HOTEL

THIS HOTEL, ONE OF THE OLDEST IN CONTINUOUS OPERA-
TION WEST OF THE ROCKIES, OPENED FOR BUSINESS IN
AUGUST, 1856. ORIGINALLY KNOWN AS THE "BICKNELL
BLOCK", THE STRUCTURE CONSISTS OF THREE COMMON-
WALLED BUILDINGS OF SIMPLE BRICK CONSTRUCTION
EMBELLISHED WITH CLASSIC REVIVAL AND WROUGHT
IRON RAILING ORNAMENTATION.

CALIFORNIA REGISTERED HISTORICAL LANDMARK NO. 899

PLAQUE PLACED BY THE STATE DEPARTMENT OF PARKS
AND RECREATION IN COOPERATION WITH THE NEVADA
COUNTY LANDMARKS COMMISSION, JUNE 30, 1976.

California Landmark

During a ceremony on June 30, 1976, in front of the National Hotel, a plaque was placed on the newly designated "California Historical Landmark No. 899" by the California Department of Parks and Recreation in cooperation with the Nevada County Landmarks Commission. The plaque, presented by Dr. Clement W. Meighan, chairman of the State Historical Resources Commission, was unveiled by Dr. Jack Rector, Dick Worth, past owner, and current owners Dick and Nan Ness. The dedication ceremonies honored the Worth and Rector families.

In August 1978 an assortment of workers set up equipment on Broad Street as part of a production crew from Hollywood hired by Cooper, Dennis and Hirsch Inc., of Los Angeles. The director, various camera men, prop people, grips, gofers and technical people descended on Nevada City and the National Hotel to shoot a television commercial for General Motors. Broad

Street was transformed Hollywood-style to look like a street in New Orleans. Two hundred smiling extras (most of them local) and some professional actors were formed into eight groups. Each group in turn would dance, sing and clap their hands to the snappy music while onlookers were lined up along the street. A five-man Dixieland band wearing straw hats and deep red vests was filmed strutting its stuff as a focal point behind a new silver Sprint DL automobile—the real star of the show. Some Dixieland band members were local residents. A second scene was shot the next day at the intersection of Main and Commercial streets before the crew packed up and headed back to Hollywood.

(L to R) Nevada City Councilman Lynn Bramkamp, Jr. (with a bass viol), Robert M. Wyckoff, (with beard and clarinet) and three SAG actors from the film company. Each earned about $135 for the day's work, plus residuals. Extras who appeared in the crowd made $35 for the 6-hour day.

21. Thomas A. Coleman Buys the National Hotel

In September 1979 Thomas Coleman bought the National from Richard and Nan Ness, seven-year owners of the hotel. The Nesses retired from the hotel business and left Nevada City for the Monterey Bay area of California.

Tom Coleman, who had been a resident of Nevada County for ten years, owned a real estate business which had been housed in the National Hotel since 1972. Coleman said he had "always liked the notion of owning the National, but never believed that he would."[1] After buying the property Coleman followed the pattern of each previous new owner: he began the immense task of redecorating, beginning with 34 of the hotel's rooms. At the time of his acquisition the hotel had a total of 60 rooms, including some that were rented out as apartments. The hotel property included three business rentals, several out-buildings and the swimming pool at the back of the property.

From the front entrance, you can view relics of the past in the glassed-in case on the left and go upstairs to the registration desk.

GRAND OPENING

The Staff and Management

Invite you to join us

for elegant dining in the

The Victorian Dining Room

Beginning at 5:30 p.m.

A complete selection of
seafood entrees, broiled steaks & chops
Continental specialties and
sumptuous desserts
Choice of appropriate wines
All prepared & served with
utmost finesse.

"THE $3.85 LUNCHEON BUFFET"
MON. – SAT. 11:30 – 2
*a regal spread of garden salads, home-
made soup, fresh roasted meats, savory
cheese. The special entrees prepared by
our chef daily.*

"A SUPER SUNDAY BRUNCH"
WKLY. 11 – 3
*champagne, assorted fresh ripe fruits,
homebaked muffins, fluffy French
omelets, quiche Apollo, eggs benedict,
buckwheat cakes, fresh roast ham.*

- AND THEN -

COME AS YOU ARE, *OR COME AS YOU WERE*
FROM 9:00 P.M. TO 12:00 A.M.

STEP BACK, ONE HUNDRED YEARS OR SO, INTO.....

.....a different time

.....a different place

....a different price

Mixed Drinks	**25¢**
Beer & Wine	**15 ¢**
Sandwiches	**5 ¢**

--PRIZES FOR BEST VICTORIAN COSTUME
--ENTERTAINMENT
--100 YEARS OF FUN

NATIONAL HOTEL

211 Broad St., Nevada City   Reservations 265-2348

This advertisement for Tom Coleman's grand opening on February 7, 1980,
appeared in *The Independent* weekly newspaper.

133

When the former owners, the Nesses, took over the hotel, their focus was to renovate the old plumbing and electrical systems to bring them up to modern standards. Coleman centered his efforts on refurbishing the guest rooms and public areas of the hotel. This is an on-going task at any busy hotel whose rooms are continually used and suffer from everyday wear.

In 1984 Coleman was given the Elza Kilroy Award at the Nevada City Chamber of Commerce annual installation dinner. Coleman had been a past chamber president, a member of the city's planning commission, and he was involved with a number of Western Nevada County clubs and civic organizations

The National Hotel's verandah was closed for almost two years, beginning the summer of 2002. Due to dry rot on the old wood balcony, the city and county deemed it structurally unsafe.

Today the Victorian dining room is located between the famous National Hotel bar and the lobby entrance.

Workers in 2002 were building a replica of the original Victorian balcony.

It was a long process for Coleman to have its replacement approved and permits secured because of conflicts between current state building codes and local requirements within the historical district. Coleman's plan called for larger beams and joists, but to maintain historical integrity, they were designed to appear identical to the old ones.

The balcony has from its beginning been a popular and important part of Broad Street's social life. Many guests book rooms at the National a year in advance in order to view the Fourth of July or Constitution Day parades—or the annual Father's Day Bicycle Classic—from this coveted vantage point. It's not surprising that the balcony has been used for more than a few weddings in the summer months.

The National Hotel's 150th Birthday

By 2006 Tom Coleman had been doing business in the historical district for almost forty years and had owned and managed the hotel for almost thirty. Like the Rectors and the Worths before him, Coleman was involved with the community and has been active in local government. In January of 2006, at the

135

Nevada City Chamber of Commerce Installation and Awards Dinner, Coleman was the recipient of the "Business Person of the Year" award.

Writers of articles about National still persisted in using erroneous dates. One article, written in 2006, incorrectly credited the National with continuous operation ever since the 1863 fire.

In 2006 the National Hotel celebrated its 150th birthday with minimal fanfare. There was an announcement in the local paper on the day of the event, and several local radio spots noted that on August 16 the National would celebrate with a dinner featuring food from the Gold Rush era. It certainly wasn't the kind of celebration the Rector Brothers would have held, but theirs was a day when people didn't have home entertainment centers or multiple (and simultaneous) events and distractions vying for their time. The celebration didn't draw hundreds of guests as in the past—in fact, the people who did attend were mainly from the local historical community, local residents who appreciated the significance and importance of the National Hotel and its impact on the community for a century and a-half.

The cost of the dinner was $18.56—a subtle allusion to the year when the National Exchange first opened its doors. The menu included Gold Rush-style camp stew, salad, sourdough bread and dessert. The anniversary event, with limited seating, was held in the National Hotel's dining room. The program included a social hour, dinner, and a program featuring guest speaker Dr. Gary Brechin. Following special music, a welcome and introductions were given by local writer and historian Max Roberts, who was master of ceremonies. Roberts gave a presentation about the National's history. Owner Tom Coleman spoke briefly, and then Nevada City Mayor Steve Cottrell, one of the city's eminent historians, introduced Dr. Brechin.

Brechin, an environmental and architectural historian with a Ph.D. in geography, and author of *Imperial San Francisco: Urban Power, Earthy Ruin*, spoke at length about the National's unique history, demonstrating his intimate knowledge of that institution. After the Brechin speech, Mayor Cottrell introduced a final song by Kim Wellman, accompanied by Noreen Barnett.

When I interviewed Tom Coleman in 2005 I asked what one

improvement he would like to make to the historic hotel, and he replied that he wanted to install an elevator. Perhaps the most important improvement during his tenure thus far has been to install fire sprinklers for added safety.

The most popular times for hotel occupancy are during the annual Constitution Day Parade in September, the Nevada City Bike Classic on Father's Day and Mardi Gras. Coleman recalled that his most memorable single event was in the 1980s, when two hundred classic cars and their owners came to the National.

Through the years dozens of famous people have stayed at the National. In its earliest days perhaps the most famous have been President Herbert Hoover and the world-renowned opera singer, Emma Nevada, who was born in the little up-county mining town of Alpha in Nevada County. More contemporary have been California Governor Jerry Brown (who stayed in the Senate Room 36) and many film stars and musical celebrities over the years.

It was a surprise to many in Nevada City when in the fall of 2006 the front page of *The Union* newspaper carried an article

Victorian period furnishings in Room 2 of the National Hotel.

headlined "Historic National Hotel for Sale, Owner says 'time to pass baton to a younger owner.'"[2] Laura Brown, staff writer for the newspaper reported that offers to buy the hotel had come in every few months since Coleman bought the place, but "it wasn't until earlier this year that be began considering them." Coleman reportedly was working to comply with state and county regulations, and was doing some minor sprucing up. The hotel probably would not go on the market for another six moths, and at that time he had not announced a selling price.

Since then the so-called Great Recession caused the nation's economy to decline, and as this book was being written in 2011, Coleman continued to own and operate the renowned National Hotel.

A popular postcard of the interior of a guest room at the National.

Golden Nuggets

- Articles about the National Hotel have appeared in many publications over the years, including the *Los Angeles Times, Sacramento Bee, Oakland Tribune, San Francisco Chronicle, Monterey Peninsula Times-Herald, Holiday* magazine, and others (even the *National Enquirer*).

- In 1887 a tri-colored pole was erected in the front of the National Hotel barber shop in honor of the visit of the Native Sons to Nevada City.

- In September 1887 a rain storm caused several men to be shocked and one man knocked off his feet. The front end of the National had iron doorways and window frames through which holes had been drilled to allow electric wires to run into the office and barroom. When the lights were turned on with the storm in progress, the ungrounded iron became heavily charged with electricity. Men standing on the wet threshold thought they had been struck by lightening. A man learning against one of the iron columns was knocked to the middle of the sidewalk. No one suffered permanent injury.

- In the Spring of 1899 improvements to the office were made that including a new glass front to the main hotel building.

- The National Hotel sponsored a baseball team called the National Hotel Club. On Sunday, April 15, 1888, the National team beat the Ridge Club at North San Juan by a score of 18 to 15.

- In the 1880s the principal inns in Nevada City were the National, New York and City hotels on Broad Street and the Union Hotel on Main Street. All were wood structures except the National.

- On January 19, 1892, some ladies at the National sent up a lighted balloon from the balcony to celebrate the election of

Stephen M. White as Unites States Senator. The balloon—which resembled a ball of fire—went up about a hundred feet and was eventually carried by the wind to the sedate neighborhood of Piety Hill.

- On January 6, 1894, the City Hotel on the corner of Broad and Union streets caught fire. The roof was destroyed and most of the second floor was damaged by fire and water. The hotel manager, O. C. Conlon, tried to put out the fire with a garden hose, but the water pipes were frozen. It was a cold morning, about 16 degrees outside, making it difficult for firefighters because the sprayed water turned to ice. After the fire was extinguished the Rector brothers invited all the firemen into the National for breakfast.

- In 1898 the Nevada County Power Company placed an electric cigar lighter in the National billiard room. It was said to be an ingenious, handy and a popular device,.

- In 1899 a live mountain lion, trapped by North San Juan resident Henry German, was presented to John Bacigalupi, bartender and boarder at the National Hotel. The cat escaped by gnawing its way out of its wooden case and found its way into a room adjoining the bar. Every night it made an appearance looking for food and "engaging in scraps with the hotel cat." The customers found great sport in watching it and throwing food to the animal.

- In April of 1903 ten carloads of firewood were delivered to the National from Buena Vista ranch via the narrow gauge railroad. In a year's time the hotel had consumed 300 cords of wood for heating and cooking. The increased usage was due to enlargement of the hotel.

- In 1903 *Leslie's Weekly*, a popular magazine of days gone by, carried an article about the wealth said to have passed across the original National Hotel bar. A story had been handed down for decades that $8 million dollars that passed over that bar in a thirty-five-year period after the Gold Rush, more than in any other saloon in the same period of time. Made of California laurel and placed in the hotel in 1864 as part of the renovation following the 1863 fire, the bar was said to have been eight inches thick when new, but heavy use had worn it down to two.

- In May 1918 federal food authorities notified local restaurants and hotel keepers that it was unlawful to have sugar bowls on the tables where patrons were served. The order was due to sugar shortages during World War I.

- In April 1934 the National Hotel was headquarters for over 100 delegates attending the 32nd annual convention of the Northern District of the Federation of Women's Clubs of California.

- In 1971 newspaper columnist and local historian Bob Paine related how his two grandmothers had declared war on federal marshals after the 1884 Sawyer Decision out-

No longer running today are the Pingalia horse-drawn carriage rides around Nevada City that started in the 1970s. Their first customer was local resident Madelyn Helling, the former county librarian for whom the Madelyn Helling Library is named.

lawed hydraulic mining. He claimed that his female relatives at Lake City were in cahoots with the desk clerks at the National in Nevada City. When federal agents came to town to enforce the Anti-Debris Act, they arrived on the Nevada County Narrow Gauge Railroad and the National bus would pick them up and take them to the hotel. Paine said agents' mode of dress (high stiff collars and black suits) and their briefcases "were dead giveaways of their evil purposes." As soon as the feds registered, desk clerks at the National would swing into action. They or someone they hired would ride a fast horse either to Paine's Hotel in Lake City or to the long-distance telephone office at French Corral to warn back-country miners that the feds would be there the next day." [3]

THE LADIES OF THE EVENING

TO COMMEMORATE THAT UBIQUITOUS SEGMENT
OF SOCIETY WHO HAVE BEEN UNACKNOWLEDGED;
WHO THOUGH OBSCURE. MADE AN ESSENTIAL
CONTRIBUTION TO THE SETTLEMENT OF THE WEST.

DEDICATED OCTOBER 7, 1972, BY
WM. BULL MEEK-WM. MORRIS STEWART
CHAPTER NO. 10 E CLAMPUS VITUS.
NEVADA CITY. CALIFORNIA

A plaque in the National Hotel parking lot sits above the Golden Center freeway, a short distance from where a business and its clients caused Mayor Rector to call it to the attention of the city council.

22. Other Fires and Fatal Facts at the National

A HOT CHIMNEY in the Wells, Fargo & Co express office in the National ignited a floor joist in the second story of the hotel on January 25, 1891, and smoke rising into room 85 almost killed R. Thomas of Birchville, who was asleep. On the third floor the connecting timbers caught fire and smoked L. A. Gates out of his room. Holes were cut in several places alongside the chimney in order to extinguish the fire.

Four years later, on January 30, 1895, a chimney at the southeast corner of the hotel caught fire. The bricks became so hot that woodwork on one of the upper stories ignited, and after a hole was cut through the floor to reach the fire, it was put out with fire extinguishers, with only slight damage to the building.

The earliest known fatality at the National was Cyrus Rowe, about age 50, a resident and former treasurer of the city of Sacramento. Rowe was a guest at the National and had been unwell for several weeks, though his condition wasn't considered to be serious. He had walked around town the day of his death, and was advised to go to bed. A physician was called, who gave him medication and assured him he would be well the next day. Later that evening Rowe told Mr. Lancaster he was dying, and he did indeed die a few minutes later, on December 12, 1858.[1]

Possibly the second death at the National was that of Mr. I. H. Sherbourne, a mining foreman and longtime resident of Omega. Sherbourne, suffering from "hemorrhage of the lung," had recently returned from San Jose, hoping the change in climate would improve his health. He was accompanied by his physician, Dr. Temple, who had attended him for quite some time. His health continued to decline until December 31, 1860, when he got up, dressed and shaved—then fell back and died.

The next known victim at the National was James Brown, who had been employed at the hotel as a porter. On Sunday, May 23, 1875, Brown was sweeping the saloon until, not feeling well, he went to his room to rest. On the following day he felt well enough to go out to the hotel's woodshed to saw wood. Mrs. Eddy ordering him to return to his room, thinking he should not be working yet. His condition worsened and he died on Tuesday.

National Hotel Annex in 1961.

A glimpse of the hotel annex from Union Street on a snowy day in the 1940s.

Appendix A. Pioneer National Hotel Men

CARR, JAMES F., was born in 1836 in Ohio, where he was a farmer until 1860, when he arrived in Nevada County. He had an interest in the Magnolia and Mountaineer mines. He married Ethel E. Mitchell and they had two sons, James F. Jr. and Lyman E. Carr. James Carr Sr. leased the National Hotel from 1865–1874. He died July 16, 1880, in Nevada City.

EDDY, COL. ALDEN H., born in Ontario (Wayne) County, New York, in 1808. Eddy married Ann Hickey of Wayne Co., New York, and they had three children, Stanley A., Ann Eliza (Mrs. Charles Adolph) and George. He farmed and operated a flour and lumber mill in New York until 1849, when he left for California on the first steamer sent out by the Pacific Mail Steamship Co. He arrived in Nevada City April 10, 1850, and first mined on Deer Creek for two years, then went to French Corral, where he, Amos Laird and others built the Shady Creek ditch and mined in the vicinity until 1873. In 1874 he bought the National Exchange Hotel. His son George went to Santa Barbara. Stanley, another son, bought a farm in Tulare county and later came back to Nevada City to manage the National Hotel. Alden H. Eddy died at the home of his daughter, Mrs. Charles Adolph, on Broad Street in November 1889.

EDDY, STANLEY A., son of Alden H. Eddy, was proprietor of the National Exchange hotel for his father in the later years until it was leased by the Rector brothers. He left Nevada County and bought a farm in Tulare County near Hanford.

GENTRY, RICHARD B., was born in Wisconsin c. 1843 and arrived in Nevada City in 1856 with his family at the age of 14. He ran for sheriff in 1865. The 23-year-old was one of the most popular young men in Nevada City and he won the election. Editorials in favor of the candidate had defended his youth and cited the fact that George Washington was an adjutant general at age 20 and Napoleon was sent to command the army of Italy at age 26. Previous to running for Sheriff, Gentry held the office of tax collector. He married Maggie Murchie, daughter of John

145

C. Murchie Sr. They had one daughter, Martha (Mattie). In 1876 Gentry moved to San Francisco to run a wholesale liquor business for about two years. After that he hired a number of Apache Indians and traveled around giving exhibitions of running and other Indian sports. After the troupe toured the East, he settled there and died in Philadelphia on April 14, 1897.

HANSON, ABEL H., an early pioneer to Nevada City, co-owned Boswell and Hanson, a grocery business on Broad Street. Abel married Caroline Mead on January 24, 1859, in Nevada City. Abel was a delegate to the Democratic convention in 1861 and a city trustee in 1858. He was a charter member of the Nevada Rifles and president of the Nevada Theatre Co. He died in San Francisco in April 1901. The Hansons lost two children to scarlet fever within a week of each other in 1864. He and his family moved to Grass Valley after he became insolvent. His wife conceived the idea for Donation Day.

HEALEY, JOSEPH, and Henry Pearson leased the U.S. Hotel at Nevada City in March 1856. After it was destroyed in the 1856 fire the pair leased the Bicknell building and converted it into the National Exchange Hotel in August. He came from Philadelphia, Pennsylvania and was married to Rachel Healey, a Quaker who became matron of the Protestant Orphan Asylum of Sacramento.

KEENEY, GEORGE, a hardware merchant and tinsmith, was born in New York, arriving in Nevada City in 1850. He was 41 years old at the time of his marriage to Elizabeth "Lizzie" Phillips on March 30, 1861 at Benicia, Calif. Two sons, George P. and Frank W., were born in Nevada City. George's wife Lizzie was also from New York. George Keeney died on Sept. 26, 1868, at this home in Nevada City of brain fever after an illness of several days. In 1870 Lizzie's mother Mary A., her sister Hattie, and a brother, George Phillips, were living with her in Nevada City.[1] By 1880 Elizabeth and her sons, along with her sister Hattie (and a Chinese servant named Ah Him) had moved to San Rafael, Calif.[2] George Keeney also owned a mine on Stocking Flat.

LANCASTER, GEORGE R., the brother of John A. Lancaster, was a hotel keeper before coming to California. He left Nevada City in 1864 to return to his native state of Maine. He visited California in 1877, attending a Pioneer Reunion in San Francisco and came up to Nevada City with Col. A. W. Potter to see those who were left from the "old days." In 1888 he died in Boston, where he had been staying after living in Maine for a number of years.

LANCASTER, JOHN A., was a Nevada City, pioneer arriving in 1852. He was born at Bangor, Maine, and died in 1873 at his home in the Grand Central Hotel in Oakland, Calif. In 1852 he and his wife Mary L. opened the Virginia boarding house on Broad Street. In 1853 he was elected vice president of the Sons of New England, representing Maine. He operated a stage service between Nevada and Forest City, and in 1855 he was the proprietor of the Union Hotel before taking over the Metropolis Livery Stables. In 1858 he was elected Nevada City trustee; in 1860 he was chairman of the fire department trustees, and in June of 1863 he was elected delegate of the Union party state convention. In March of 1864 he and his brother-in-law, Samuel Hasey, leased the rebuilt National Exchange Hotel. Lancaster bought Hasey's interest in the hotel in December 1869. He was the brother of George R. Lancaster.

PEARSON, HENRY H., came to California with his brother, Edward L. Pearson. In 1855 the brothers were proprietors of the Fountain Restaurant on Main Street in Nevada City. He and Joseph Healey leased the U.S. Hotel, and then opened the National Exchange Hotel in Bicknell's Block after the 1865 fire. In 1865 Pearson moved to San Francisco where he managed the American Exchange Hotel and later the Russ House. In October 1887 he moved to Southern California to mange the Arcadia Hotel in Santa Monica.

YOUNG, GEORGE A., a forty-niner and early resident of Nevada City, died in April 1884 at Oakland, California. In 1855 he resided in and owned a brick building east of Bicknell's Block, and after the fire of 1856 his lot and gutted building became part of the National Exchange Hotel. He and his brother-in-law, William F. Anderson, were injured in that fire. Young was so severely burned that he lost the use of one of his hands. His face was burned so badly that for a long time it was believed he might not recover. He did, however, and moved to San Francisco, where in September 1875 he was elected to the state assembly.

Appendix B. California State Historical Landmarks Located in Nevada County

#134. Donner of Pioneer Monument (Truckee)

#247. First Long-Distance Telephone in the World (French Corral)

#292. Lola Montez House Replica (Grass Valley)

#293. Crabtree House (Grass Valley)

#294. Rough and Ready (Rough and Ready)

#297. Gold Quartz Discovery (Grass Valley)

#298. Empire Mine (Grass Valley)

#390. Bridgeport Covered Bridge (South Yuba River)

#628–9. Alpha and Omega Hydraulic Diggings (Omega rest area on Highway 20)

#780–6. First Transcontinental Railroad (Truckee)

#799. Overland Emigrant Trail—Highway 49 (South Wolf Creek bridge on Highway 49)

#832. South Yuba Canal Office (Nevada City)

#843. North Star Mine Powerhouse (Grass Valley)

#852. North Bloomfield Mining and Gravel Company (Malakoff Diggins State Park, North Bloomfield)

#855. Mount Saint Mary's Convent and Academy (Grass Valley)

#863. Nevada Theatre (Nevada City)

#899. National Exchange Hotel (Nevada City)

#914. The Holbrooke Hotel (Grass Valley)

#1102. Pelton Wheel Manufacturing Site (Nevada City)

Notes

FRONT MATTER / pages i–xviii

1. This old advertisement was reprinted in *The Independent* newspaper on May 30, 1977, p. 12.
2. *Nevada Nugget*, May 1, 1963. "The National Hotel, A Nevada City Landmark," p. 1.
3. *Western Living*, "The Reminiscences of Dan Fletcher," annotated by Doris Foley, September 13, 1968, shows a diagram of "The Fire at Nevada City" taken from a San Francisco newspaper, July 27, 1856, and lists 33 brick buildings.
4. *Nevada Transcript* (Nevada City) July 7, 1896, p. 2.
5. Evidently Mr. Gault's vote was a "no" vote on Ordinance No. 129.

CHAPTER 1 / pages 1–6

1. Van Orman, Richland A. *A Room for the Night: Hotels of the Old West.* Bonanza Book, New York, 1966, p. 4.
2. Cross, Ralph Herbert. *The Early Inns of California 1844-1869.* Cross & Brandt, San Francisco, 1954, p. 173.
3. *Nevada Journal,* April 19, 1851.
4. Sargent, Aaron. "Sketch of Nevada County." *Brown & Dallison's Nevada, Grass Valley and Rough and Ready Directory.* San Francisco: Town Talk Office, pp. 20–21.
5. Tyson, Edwin L., [Title?] Nevada County Historical Society *Bulletin* April 2006, p. 2.
6. Wilson, Luzena Stanley. *Luzena Stanley Wilson '49er.* The Eucalyptus Press, Mills College, CA, April 1937, p. 27.

CHAPTER 2 / pages 7–11

1. Comstock, David A. *150 Years Ago* (Grass Valley, Nevada City, Truckee, CA) Nevada County Sesquicentennial, 1998, p. 7
2. *Nevada Journal*, Feb. 25, 1853, p. 3. Proclamation advertisement.

CHAPTER 3 / pages 12–15

1. *Nevada Transcript,* Aug. 26, 1862, p. 1.
2. *Nevada Journal,* Sept. 18, 1851, p. 3.
3. Charles D. Ferguson. *The Experiences of a Forty-niner During Thirty-four Year's Residence in California and Australia.* Cleveland, Ohio: The Williams Publishing Co., 1888, pp. 148–49.
4. *Nevada Journal,* July 3, 1852, p. 2, c. 2.
5. Some sources give the date as Sept. 4, 1852, and it may have been a typographical error.
6. Wells, Harry L., et. al. *History of Nevada County, California.* Oakland: Thompson and West, 1880, p.81. Berkeley: Howell-North, 1970. p. 84.

7. Although a later deed in 1856 from David W. Aldrich to P. V. Skillman notes that "Alddrich [sic] purchased the property from Hussey in December 29, 1855," this date must come from faulty memory. A short article in the *Nevada Journal* of September 22, 1854 says "Mr. [David] Aldrich has purchased the popular Metropolis Hotel from Mr. [Simon] Hussey."

8. Nevada County Deed Book 1, p. 62, 4 June 1856.

CHAPTER 4 / pages 16–18

1. *Nevada Journal*, "Brick Yards," Jan. 16, 1857, p. 2.

2. Foley, Doris. *Western Living.* Chart from *The Golden Era*, July 27, 1856. Sept 13, 1968, p. 10.

CHAPTER 5 / pages 19–28

1. *Nevada Journal*, "Fire Proof Buildings in Nevada." March 7, 1856, p. 2.

2. Foley, Doris. *Western Living.* Chart from *The Golden Era*, July 27, 1856. Sept. 13, 1968, p. 10.

3. Officer, Lawrence H., and Samuel H. Williamson. "Purchasing Power of Money in the United States from 1774 to 2010," http://measuringworth. com (using 2010 data).

CHAPTER 6 / pages 29–31

1. *Nevada Journal*, "New Hotel," Aug. 22, 1856, p. 3.

2. *Nevada Journal*, National Exchange adv., Aug. 15, 1856, p. 3.

3. Nevada Journal, "City Election," May 8, 1857, p. 2.

4. 1856 *Brown & Dallison's Nevada, Grass Valley and Rough and Ready Directory*, reprinted by Maria E. Brower, 2001, p. 78.

5. E-mail from David A. Comstock, Nov. 2, 2009. to Maria Brower.

6. *Nevada Journal*, "Fire and Water," Sept. 4, 1857. p. 2.

7. Glen Conner. "History of Weather Observations, The Presidio of San Francisco, California 1847–1892." April 2005. http://mrcc.isws.illinois. edu/FORTS/histories/CA_Presidio of San Francisco Conner.pdf. 11/11/09.

CHAPTER 7 / pages 32–35

1. *Nevada Journal*, "Credit to Whom it is Due," May 28, 1858, p. 2

2. *Nevada Journal,* "Plank and Turnpike Road," Jan. 15, 1858, p. 2.

CHAPTER 8 / pages 36–42

1. *Nevada Democrat*, National Exchange adv., Sept. 22, 1858, p. 3.

2. *Nevada Daily Transcript*, "Going to Rebuild," Nov. 13, 1863 p. 2.

3. *Nevada Daily Transcript*, "List of Losses," Nov. 13, 1863, p., 2.

4. Wells, Harry L., et. al. *History of Nevada County, California.* Oakland: Thompson and West, 1880, Berkeley: Howell-North, 1970, p. 86.

5. *Nevada Daily Transcript*, "The Town," Nov. 28, 1863, p. 2.

6. *Nevada Daily Transcript*, "List of Losses," Nov. 10, 1863, p. 2.

7. *Nevada Daily Transcript*, "The Water Question, Again," Jan. 13, 1864, p. 2.

8. *Nevada Daily Transcript*, "Nevada Hose Co., No. 1," Jan. 13, 1864, p. 3.

9. Nevada County 1863 Assessment Book, Nevada City Township, p. 32.

10. *Nevada Daily Transcript*, "The Courthouse Bell," Nov. 25, 1863, p. 3.

CHAPTER **9** / pages 43–49
1. *Nevada Daily Transcript*, "The Hotels," Dec. 25, 1863, p. 3.
2. *Ibid.*
3. *Nevada Daily Transcript*, "The National," April 2, 1864, p. 3.

CHAPTER **10** / pages 50–53
1. *The Daily Union* (Grass Valley), "The Sunday Law," Jan. 26, 1873, p. 2.
2. *Ibid.*
3. *Nevada Daily Transcript*, "The Sunday Law," March 14, 1882, p. 2.

CHAPTER **12** / pages 58–67
1. Irvine, Leigh H. *History of New California: Its Resources and People.* Lewis Publishing, 1905, p. 935.
2. *Nevada City Nugget.* Aug. 16, 1961, sec 2, p. 4.
3. *The Union* (Grass Valley), "Poorman Relates More Stories About Hydraulic Mining Days," Dec. 5, 1960, p. 2.
4. *Nevada City Nugget*, "California's Oldest Hotel?" April 24, 1963, p. 1.
5. *The Transcript*, "Ordinance No. 129 Section 62," July 7, 1896, p. 2.
6. *Nevada Daily Transcript*, "A Few Inducements Which Nevada County Offers to Settlers," March 6, 1894, p. 3.

CHAPTER **13** / pages 68–75
1. *The Transcript*, "The Remodeled Courthouse," Feb. 13, 1900, p 3.
2. *The Union*, "The Trail: Three Adjuncts of Great Aid to Fire Dept," April 23, 1960, p. 1.
3. *The Transcript*, "It is a Noted Bar," March 17, 1900, p. 3.
4. *The Daily Morning Union*, "Bawdy Houses to Be Suppressed," Dec. 4, 1900, p. 4.
5. *The Daily Morning Union*, "News Notes Condensed," Dec. 6, 1900, p. 4.
6. *Nevada Daily Transcript*, "A Popular Hotel," March 16, 1901, p. 5.

CHAPTER **14** / pages 76–84
1. *The Morning Union*, "Held Superior Court in National Hotel Parlor," April 3, 1912, p. 1.
2. *The Union,* "B. S. Rector Stilled by Death," May 2, 1915, p. 1.
3. Larder, W. B., and M. J. Brock, *History of Placer and Nevada County,* 1924, p. 1003 (biography of Edward D. Leichter).

CHAPTER **15** / pages 85–96
1. *The Union*, "Coffee Shop to Oust 40 Year Old Barber Shop at National," Jan. 31, 1926, p. 5.
2. *The Union*, "National Hotel Coffee Shop Is Completed and Ready to Serve," March 26, 1926, p. 5.
3. *The Union*, "Nevada City's National Hotel Fire Damaged," Nov. 27, 1928, pp. 1–2.
4. *Grass Valley Union*, December 30, 1930, p. 1 (quoted in *The 1930s: No Depression Here*, p. 131).
5. *The Morning Union*, "Hotel Guide Warm in Praise of Grass Valley As Hospitality Center," Jan. 3, 1929, p. 5.

6. Grant Deed from L. B. Lutz to F. G. Worth et ux, 20 June 1929 (recorded 25 June 1929) Nevada County, California Deed Bk. 2, p. 241.

7. *The Morning Union,* "National Hotel Register of 57 Years Ago's Old Names Album," Apr. 18, 1930, p. 2.

8. *The Morning Union,* "Fred C. Worth Becomes Sole Owner of National; Lola M. Worth Retires," March 19, 1933, p. 2.

CHAPTER **16** / pages 97–102

1. *The Nugget,* "National Hotel Sold to George E. Murphy," Oct. 31, 1946, pp. 1, 8.

2. *The Union,* "National Hotel In Receivership For Sale Suit," July 14, 1950, p. 1.

3. *Nevada City Nugget,* "National Hotel Sold to George E. Murphy," Oct. 31, 1946, p. 1, 8.

4. *The Union,* "New Post Office Opens," Dec. 9, 1972, p. 1.

5. *Nevada City Nugget,* "National Hotel Menu Sought By Collectors," Nov. 4, 1946, p. 7.

6. Memorandum of Lease, Sept 15. 1947, recorded in Nevada County Original Records Book, 117, p. 478–9.

7. *Nevada City Nugget,* "Meet Mr. Huckins, the New Owner of the National Hotel," Oct. 10, 1947, p. 1

8. *Nevada City Nugget,* "National is Taken Over By New Owners," Feb. 3, 1950. p. 1.

9. Nevada County Recorder's Office, Nevada City. Official records checked from 1927–1970.

10. *The Union,* "National Hotel in Receivership for Sale Suit." July 14, 1950, p. 1.

11. *Ibid.*

12. Certificate of Sale on Foreclosure by Commissioner, Richard Worth et al vs George Murphy et al Jan. 27, 1951 (recorded Jan. 29, 1951) Nevada Cit. Vol. 158, pp. 332–334 Nevada County Recorder's Officce.

13. *The Union,* "National Hotel, Ancient Landmark, Makes Comeback With Remodeling and Addition of Fine Museum," April 13, 1951, p. 2.

14. *The Union,* "National is Great Grandpappy of Elegantly-restored Hotels," Sept. 1969 p. 10.

15. *The Independent,* "People," October 20, 1976, p. 5.

16. *The Nugget,* "Pictorial Progress: Pioneer," Aug. 22, 1962, Sec. D p. 1.

CHAPTER **17** / pages 103–106

1. *The Union,* "Old Style Eating Plan to Start Friday Night," Aug. 17, 1953, p. 2.

CHAPTER **18** / pages 107–117

1. *The Union,* "Haddy Predicts Boom in 60s at Chamber Dinner," Jan. 20, 1960, p. 2.

2. *Ibid.*

3. *California History,* Fall 1980 p. 208.

4. *The Union,* "Freeway Route, Attractive to NC, Not Offensive, Gets Solid Support After 'No Choice' Fully Explained," Oct. 29, 1960, p. 2.

5. *Ibid.*

6. Wells, Harry L., et al. *History of Nevada County, California,* Oakland: Thompson and West, 1880, p. 55.

7. *The Union,* "Little Park of NC Prominent in City's History," Aug. 24, 1963, p. 3.

8. *The Union,* "The Tale of a Freeway that Divided Two Cities," by Bob Wyckoff, Feb. 22, 2003, p. C7.

9. *The Union,* "City Planners Want No Part of Freeway Fight," Oct. 5, 1960, p. 2.

10. *Nevada County Nugget,* "Freeway War Ends, Compromise Design Adopted by City," May 29, 1963, pp. 1, 3.

11. *Nevada City Nugget,* "Scenic Freeway is Acceptable," May 15, 1963, pp. 1–3.

12. *The Union,* "Nevada Cityans—Don't Throw Your 100 Years Stability Into the Decay of Closed Stores—They're Not Quaint," Nov. 19, 1960, p. 2.

13. *The Union,* "Bypassing Nevada City Could Lead to Economic Stagnation, Vote Tomorrow is Important," Nov. 21, 1960, p. 8.

14. *The Union,* "Freeway Route, as Proposed by State, Approved," Nov. 23, 1960, p. 2.

15. *The Union,* "Brockington Retires from Golden Center," May 12, 1918, p. 8.

CHAPTER **19** / pages 118–123

1. *The Union,* "Holbrook [sic] Hotel Is Now the Grass Valley," Aug. 7, 1918, p. 3.

2. *Nevada City Nugget,* Nov. 9, 1960, p. 8.

3. *The Union,* Oct. 22, 1960, p. 2.

4. *The Union,* "Flames Damage National Annex," Dec. 12, 1960, p. 2.

5. *Nevada City Nugget,* "Photo Studio Boarded," Dec. 14, 1960, p. 1.

6. *Ibid.*

7. *Nevada City Nugget,* "Sunset Magazine to Feature N.C.," Aug. 9, 1961, p. 1.

8. *The Union,* "Plaque to be Placed on Old National Hotel in Clamper Ceremony," May 3, 1963, p. 2.

CHAPTER **20** / pages 124–131

1. *The Union,* "NC gets Historical District," Aug. 13, 1968, p. 1.

2. *The Union,* "National is Great Grandpappy of Elegantly-restored Hotels," Sept. 24, 1969. p. 10.

3. *The Union,* "Dick Worth Appreciation Dinner at National Hotel," Sept. 30, 1972, p. 1.

4. *The Independent,* "New Bus Stop," April 19, 1975, p. 34.

5. *Ibid.*

6. *Nevada City Nugget,* "A literal gold mine? National Hotel moves into its 122 year," Jan. 15, 1976, p. 2.

7. *Ibid.*

CHAPTER **21** / pages 132–142

1. *The Union,* "National Hotel, NC landmark renovation to continue," Oct. 5, 1979, p. 15.

2. *The Union,* Oct. 26, 2006, pp. 1, 12.

3. *The Union* "Humbug—The Story of a Conflict," by Bob Paine, June 2, 1971, p. 6.

CHAPTER **22** / pages 143–144

1. *Nevada Democrat*, "Sudden Death," Dec. 15, 1858, p. 3.

APPENDIX A / pages 145–147s

1. 1870 U.S. Federal Population Census, Nevada Township, Nevada City, Nevada County, CA, p. 287.

2. 1880 US Federal Population Census, San Rafael, Marin County, CA p. 112B.

Drawings found under old wallpaper when refurbishing the National Hotel.

Bibliography

COMSTOCK, DAVID A., ED AND COMP. *150 Years Ago*. Grass Valley, Nevada City, Truckee, CA: Nevada County Sesquicentennial Committee, 1998.

CROSS, RALPH HERBERT. *The Early Inns of California 1844–1869*. San Francisco: Cross & Brandt, 1954.

FERGUSON, CHARLES D. *The Experiences of a Forty-niner During Thirty-four Year's Residence in California and Australia*. Cleveland, Ohio: The Williams Publishing Co., 1888.

IRVINE, LEIGH H. *History of New California: Its Resources and People*. New York & Chicago: Lewis Publishing, 1905.

LARDNER, W. B., AND M. J. BROCK. *History of Placer and Nevada Counties, California, with BIographical Sketches*. Los Angeles: Historic Record Company, 1924.

RECTOR, JOHN MOTT, M.D., *Eleven Generations of the Rector Family in the United States of America*. Nevada City, CA, 1976.

SARGENT, AARON A., "Sketch of Nevada County." *Brown & Dallison's Nevada, Grass Valley and Rough and Ready Directory*. San Francisco: Town Talk Office, 1856. Reprinted by Maria E. Brower, 2001.

VAN ORMAN, RICHLAND A., *A Room for the Night: Hotels of the Old West*. New York: Bonanza Books, 1966.

WELLS, HARRY L., ET. AL., *History of Nevada County, California*. Oakland: Thompson and West, 1880. Reprinted Berkeley: Howell-North, 1970.

WILSON, LUZENA STANLEY. *Luzena Stanley Wilson '49er*. Mills College, CA: The Eucalyptus Press, 1937.

Index

156